PENGUIN PASSNOTES

She Stoops to Conquer

GW01417746

Andrew Swarbrick graduated with first-class honours in English from Leeds University, where he also studied for his research degree and gained his teaching qualification. He has published articles and reviews in various academic journals and edited a volume of essays entitled *The Art of Oliver Goldsmith* (Vision Press, London, 1984). He is Director of Studies at a tutorial college in Birmingham.

PENGUIN PASSNOTES

OLIVER GOLDSMITH

She Stoops to Conquer

ANDREW SWARBRICK, B.A., M.PHIL, P.G.C.E.
ADVISORY EDITOR: STEPHEN COOTE, M.A., PH.D

PENGUIN BOOKS

Penguin Books Ltd, Harmondsworth, Middlesex, England
Viking Penguin Inc., 40 West 23rd Street, New York, New York 10010, U.S.A.
Penguin Books Australia Ltd, Ringwood, Victoria, Australia
Penguin Books Canada Ltd, 2801 John Street, Markham, Ontario, Canada L3R 1B4
Penguin Books (N.Z.) Ltd, 182 190 Wairau Road, Auckland 10, New Zealand

First published 1986

Made and printed in Great Britain by
Richard Clay (The Chaucer Press) Ltd, Bungay, Suffolk
Filmset in 10/12pt Monophoto Ehrhardt by
Northumberland Press Ltd, Gateshead

Contents

To the Student

This book is designed to help you with your O-level, C.S.E. or 16+ English Literature examination. It contains a synopsis of the plot, a glossary of the more unfamiliar words and phrases, and a commentary on some of the issues raised by the text. An account of the writer's life is also included for background.

Page references in parentheses are to the Penguin text of *She Stoops to Conquer* in *Four English Comedies*, edited by J. M. Morrell.

When you use this book remember that it is no more than an aid to your study. It will help you find passages quickly and perhaps give you some ideas for essays. But remember: *this book is not a substitute for reading the text and it is your knowledge and your response that matter.* These are the things the examiners are looking for, and they are also the things that will give you the most pleasure. Show your knowledge and appreciation to the examiner, and show them clearly.

Oliver Goldsmith

It is somehow typical of Oliver Goldsmith's accident-prone life that even his date of birth should be uncertain: the year was torn away from the family Bible where it was entered. He was born at Pallas, Co. Westmeath in Ireland, on 10 November around the year 1730, the fifth child of the Rev. Charles Goldsmith and his wife Ann. His father was at this time curate to the rector of Kilkenny West and also farmed a few fields. Shortly after his birth the family moved to Lissoy, where Goldsmith spent his childhood.

He attended a number of schools, where he proved himself quite a capable boy but he was often unhappy, particularly after a bout of smallpox disfigured his appearance (about which he was very sensitive all his life) and made him the target of schoolboy cruelty. His family was too poor to pay for his fees as a student at Trinity College, Dublin, so he obtained a place there as a sizar, acting as a college servant performing menial tasks and made conspicuous by his sizar's cap and gown. His tutor often bullied him and, after he was punished for his part in a student escapade, he ran away, but lack of money forced him to return.

Goldsmith scraped through his B.A. degree in 1749 or 1750 and for a time led an unsettled life. After various schemes fell through he set out in 1752 for Edinburgh to study medicine. He liked neither Scotland nor the Scots and in 1753 decided to complete his medical studies at Leyden in Holland. By February 1755 he had once more grown restless and with one clean shirt and next to no money he set out to tour Europe, travelling chiefly on foot and often paying his way by entertaining his peasant hosts with his flute playing.

By February 1756 he was in London, aimless and destitute. It has been conjectured that he tried acting for a short time. Much more certain is that he became assistant to a chemist and then managed to set up as a physician. He did badly. Friends later told the story of how he took pains to carry his hat so as to conceal a patch in his coat. About the end of 1756 he became usher or assistant master in a school at Peckham run by Dr Milner, but the experience was shortlived, for Goldsmith could control neither the boys nor his own impulsive spending. Dr Milner died shortly after Goldsmith had joined him, the unfortunate intention having been that Goldsmith was also to provide medical care for Dr Milner. However, at Milner's house, Goldsmith met a bookseller named Griffiths who owned a major periodical of the day called the *Monthly Review*. Early in 1757, Goldsmith agreed to lodge with Griffiths and to work for the periodical at a modest salary. From April 1757 Goldsmith contributed articles and reviews on a wide range of subjects, and thus began his literary career. But he was unhappy with what he considered to be Griffiths's exploitation of him and he applied for a post as doctor in the service of the East India Company. On 21 December 1758, he was examined at Surgeons' Hall for a certificate as 'hospital mate'. Having borrowed a suit of clothes from Griffiths to look his best, he failed the exam.

Goldsmith was forced to rely on hack-work, writing essays and reviews to earn himself some sort of living. His first success came in 1759 with *An Enquiry into the Present State of Polite Learning in Europe*, a not very penetrating study of European culture which nevertheless attracted the notice of a few influential writers and editors who put more work Goldsmith's way. He began to make some useful acquaintances: Thomas Percy (1729–1811), afterwards bishop of Dromore and Goldsmith's first biographer, visited him and shared his interest in old ballads. Tobias Smollett (1721–71), who was at this time connected with the influential *Critical Review*, was able to give Goldsmith work. By 1760, Goldsmith was hard at work contributing to three new periodicals, the most interesting being *The Bee*, to which Goldsmith was the principal if not the sole contributor. Given such circumstances, it is not surprising it only lasted through eight weekly numbers. But Goldsmith had formed an important connection with John Newbery, a bookseller who, in 1760, began a newspaper called *The Public Ledger*. He engaged Goldsmith to contribute articles twice a week and Goldsmith began a series of letters supposedly written by a Chinese visitor to London, who comments with the detachment of an outsider on all sorts of aspects of English life. During 1760, ninety-eight letters appeared in all and proved popular as well as gaining wide admiration. Goldsmith's literary reputation grew; in May 1761 he met the great Dr Johnson and the two men remained friends for life. In 1762, his 'Chinese Letters' were collected and published as *The Citizen of the World*.

He continued working hard at essays, short biographies, reviews and generally admired poems such as *The Traveller*, but whatever money he earned had already been spent on lavish hospitality, gaudy clothes and simple generosity. In March 1766 his most famous prose work, *The Vicar of Wakefield*, was published. Johnson's biographer, James Boswell, tells the story that Johnson was one morning called in by Goldsmith, whose landlady had arrested him for failing to pay his rent. Finding Goldsmith's novel ready for the press, Johnson took it to a publisher, sold it for around £60 and brought back the money which enabled Goldsmith to pay his debt. Thus was born one of the most enduring works in English fiction.

His reputation continued to increase and his works grew more generally popular, although his first play, *The Good-Natured Man*, was badly received on its opening night in January 1768. His poem *The Deserted Village* (May 1770) was, however, an immediate triumph. He wrote *She Stoops to Conquer* quickly in 1771, although it was not performed until two years later. In his last years Goldsmith was widely known and much beloved, although never free of money worries. The years of constant work and financial pressures took their toll and on 25 March 1774, he fell ill with a kidney infection. He died on 4 April 1774. His friends organized his burial and paid for the monument in Westminster Abbey which carries an inscription by Johnson in Latin; we may translate it: 'There was no kind of writing almost that he did not touch; none that he touched that he did not adorn.'

Goldsmith puzzled his contemporaries. He was unpredictable, vain and sometimes foolish. He hated being overlooked in company, was sometimes an embarrassment to his friends, and frequently spoke without much idea of what he was saying. But there was no trace of malice in his character, his charity was endless, his kindness infallible and his humane wisdom matched the more educated intellect of any man of his day. In some ways he was an oddity, but the grace, ease and elegance of his writing have won the admiration of generations of readers.

Introduction to
She Stoops to Conquer

It has been calculated that barely a month goes by without, somewhere, *She Stoops to Conquer* being performed on the professional or amateur stage. It has been successful ever since it was first produced in 1773. It ran for twelve nights at a time when plays came and went in a couple of days, producing £400 or £500 for its author (a considerable sum at that time) and it has been published in innumerable editions.

In order to appreciate fully Goldsmith's dramatic achievements, we need to place his work in the context of eighteenth-century drama as a whole. With the restoration of Charles II to the throne in 1660 came the reopening of theatres, which had been closed by the Puritan government. Courtly and aristocratic tastes, largely moulded in France, dominated theatrical fashion. In reaction to Puritan strictness, the demand was now for plays of sexual intrigue, with rakes and libertines stalking the stage, wooing the wives of gullible husbands and cynically manipulating all those standing in the way of pleasure and conquest. Two plays which worthily survive from this period are William Wycherley's *The Country Wife* (1672) and William Congreve's *The Way of the World* (1700). But by the turn of the century, taste was shifting once again. With the rise of the middle class came a demand for a drama less licentious and more morally uplifting, more refined and genteel. So arose a school of dramatists whose main aim was to use the theatre as an agent of moral reform. Plays became timid and insipid, sacrificing character and situation for the simplistic comforts of moral improvement. Acting and preaching were identical. A few plays were more robust, particularly in satirizing politicians of the 1720s and 1730s, but the Licensing Act of 1737 limited the number of London theatres to two and submitted all plays to censorship.

Goldsmith's friend David Garrick, who was actor-manager of the Drury Lane theatre, tried to shift his audience's taste by introducing some theatrical reforms. Instead of actors declaiming their lines as if they were merely reciting poetry, Garrick used facial expression and gestures which helped convey emotion. He resurrected interest in Shakespeare and placed increased emphasis on costume and scenery and took artificial lighting effects into consideration. He thus gave dramatists much greater scope for the creation of lively incident and more naturalistic dialogue and characterization.

Goldsmith himself strongly disapproved of much of the drama of his day, particularly the type known as 'sentimental comedy'. Here we enter a genteel stage world in which masculine virtue or feminine delicacy is threatened by some unscrupulous villain. The hero or heroine endures torment with well-bred indignation until the fifth act, when their virtue happily conquers all, either by force of its own merit or rescued by implausibly good fortune. Plays of this type are nowadays unreadable: they are unbearably artificial, conventional and melo-dramatic. Goldsmith was one of a few dramatists who recovered genuine 'laughing' comedy based on the credible foibles and failings of recognizable human beings. We need to remember that in writing *She Stoops to Conquer* Goldsmith was not only amusing his audience, but risking his own reputation.

She Stoops to Conquer was not Goldsmith's first play. Early in 1767 he offered *The Good-Natured Man* to David Garrick for the Drury Lane theatre. Although relations between them were usually warm, the two men had quarrelled some years earlier and after Garrick expressed doubts about the play's success, Goldsmith offered it to George Colman, the manager of Covent Garden, who accepted it. The planned first performance was delayed because Garrick, in competition, brought out a sentimental comedy by Hugh Kelly, called *False Delicacy*. This appealed to the audience's taste for sombre, rather tear-jerking plays exhibiting middle-class characters and the simple triumph of good over evil. (This fashionable vogue is mockingly referred to in the Prologue to *She Stoops to Conquer* which Garrick wrote for Goldsmith as a gesture of reconciliation.) When *The Good-Natured Man* was finally performed on 29 January 1768 it met with a mixed reception, particularly in the case of one scene, which portrayed some bailiffs. The audience, shocked by the intrusion of lower-class characters on to the stage, booed and hissed in derisive disapproval. (This helps to explain why, in *She Stoops to Conquer*, Goldsmith has his country bumpkins in the Three Pigeons jokingly disapprove of 'anything that's low'. Goldsmith is, in effect, getting his own back on his audience.)

His first play, then, was not a happy experience and Goldsmith experienced similar problems in the preparations for *She Stoops to Conquer*. It was offered to George Colman in 1772 but, not unnaturally, he hesitated, and was finally forced to yield to pressure brought to bear on him by Goldsmith's influential friend Dr Johnson. Actors declined parts and Goldsmith had great problems in arranging for a suitable epilogue. Finally, the play was performed at Covent Garden on 15 March 1773. Goldsmith was dreadfully nervous and remained outside the theatre. Johnson organized a body of friends inside to lead the audience's laughter and applause. There was no need: it was an immediate success. Goldsmith said he wrote the play simply to make an audience merry and it has been doing so for two hundred years.

The reading of a play can be a disappointing experience, particularly when it is as fast-moving and as genuinely funny as *She Stoops to Conquer* is. The best way to appreciate the play is to see it in performance. Failing that, you must try to create your own stage in your imagination. Try to imagine the appearance of the characters: Hastings and Marlow in their colourful, expensive finery; Mr Hardcastle in his long wig and drab old waistcoat; Mrs Hardcastle in lurid costume and hair piled mountainously on her head. The most important thing is to try to imagine how the dialogue might be spoken, the tone of voice suggested by the words, the comic confusion experienced by the characters. If you can bring the play to life, you will enjoy it as generations have done already.

Synopsis

We are introduced first to Mr and Mrs Hardcastle, who are arguing. Mrs Hardcastle is complaining about the dull life they lead in their old, rambling house. She badly wants to visit London to catch up on the latest fashions, but her husband hates the follies and vanities of London which so infect the modern age. He loves everything old and is happy to live simply, in rural seclusion. The argument turns to Tony Lumpkin, Mrs Hardcastle's son by her first marriage. Mr Hardcastle is exasperated by his stepson's childish behaviour, but his wife, who clearly dotes on Tony, tries to excuse him saying that he is a delicate young man.

Tony himself noisily enters (238). He is the picture of rude health and is anxious to get away to the village inn, the Three Pigeons. His mother tries to detain him, but Tony is not to be stopped and bundles her out of the way. Clearly, he is not a delicate young man at all.

Mr Hardcastle despairs of his wife and stepson. His only hope lies in his daughter, Kate, who he hopes will resist falling prey to the modern obsession with fashion and finery. Kate enters wearing her fashionable clothes and she reminds her father of their arrangement whereby she is allowed to dress as she pleases in the morning, but will wear a plain dress in the evening to please him. Mr Hardcastle tells her that he is expecting the arrival of Mr Marlow, the son of his old friend Sir Charles Marlow, whom he has chosen as his daughter's future husband. (Marriages were often arranged in this way.) He says that the young man is intelligent, generous, brave and very handsome, all of which delights Kate. The final recommendation is that he is remarkably reserved and modest in his manner. This does not please Kate at all, but she decides to judge him for herself (241).

Mr Hardcastle goes to prepare the servants for Marlow's arrival, leaving Kate to discuss Marlow with her cousin Constance Neville, Mrs Hardcastle's niece and ward. Constance knows of him through her own lover, Mr Hastings, for Marlow and Hastings are close friends. She tells Kate of Marlow's curious reputation. He is awkward and bashful in the presence of well-bred women of his own class, but very different among less refined women of a lower rank. Kate is surprised, but lets the matter go at that and turns the conversation to Constance's affairs. She has just come from Mrs Hardcastle, who is determined that her niece shall marry her son, Tony, to keep Constance's fortune, which mainly comprises her jewels, in the family. For the moment, Constance is prepared to pretend to Mrs Hardcastle that she has some feelings for Tony, to disguise from her aunt her secret love for Hastings, to whom she was betrothed by her deceased father. Kate tells her that there is no danger of Tony ever falling in love with Constance. Both girls are aware that their marital fortunes must soon be settled. Their conversation is interrupted by Mrs Hardcastle's bell summoning them to their constitutional walk (242).

The second scene shifts the location to the Three Pigeons where Tony is having fun with his friends. He sings them a song and is promising them the fun they will have once he inherits his fortune, when he is interrupted by the landlord who tells him that two strangers have lost their way *en route* to Mr Hardcastle's house. Tony, guessing that one of them must be the gentleman coming to court his sister Kate, tells the landlord to invite them in and clears his friends away (245). Alone for a moment, he wonders whether he dare revenge himself on his stepfather by playing a trick on him.

Marlow and Hastings enter, tired and rather out of sorts after their tiresome journey. They are curt and abrupt with Tony, thinking that he is a local country bumpkin. When, in answer to Tony's questions, Marlow refers to him by reputation as 'an awkward booby' (246), Tony determines to play his trick. With the landlord's help, he disconcerts the two visitors by inventing long, complicated instructions to reach Mr Hardcastle's house. They do not relish the prospect of being lost in the country at night, so Tony directs them to the nearest comfortable 'inn', the 'Buck's Head'. In reality this is Mr Hardcastle's house, and in order to allay the two visitors' suspicions once they meet Mr Hardcastle, Tony tells them to expect an unusual innkeeper who likes to think himself a gentleman. Tony leads the two gentlemen on their way.

Act II returns us to Mr Hardcastle's house, where Mr Hardcastle is attempting to train his servants, who are not used to company, to perform their duties properly when his guest, Marlow, arrives. He does not have much success. He leaves on hearing a coach draw up and his hapless recruits scatter in alarm.

Marlow and Hastings enter, commenting favourably on the 'inn'. Marlow is used to such places for he is well-travelled, and his friend expresses his surprise that Marlow has not yet acquired ease of manner in the presence of ladies. Marlow explains that, with studying or travelling, most of his life has been spent beyond the company of well-bred women, so he has never felt confident when encountering them. However, with women of a different sort, he is much more familiar (251). He explains to Hastings that he expects nothing of his meeting with Kate Hardcastle and that his main purpose is to help introduce his friend to the Hardcastles and to aid Hastings's suit with Constance.

Their conversation is interrupted by Mr Hardcastle, come to give them a hearty welcome. Marlow briefly responds, and then turns to discuss with Hastings what clothes they should wear to meet the ladies next day. Mr Hardcastle, unaware of what they are talking about, tries to join in the conversation, only to be rebuffed by the young men's inattentiveness. They behave exactly as they would do at an inn, and call for a glass of punch. Surprised, Mr Hardcastle does as he is commanded. He calls for a toast with a familiarity which in turn surprises the young men. There follows a confused conversation in which the characters talk at cross-purposes and so remain in ignorance. Marlow then calls for the supper menu. In some astonishment, Mr Hardcastle sends a servant for the menu which, when shown to Marlow and Hastings, does nothing to please them, for the food is far too rich and elaborate for their tastes. Marlow then proposes that they inspect their accommodation. Mr Hardcastle, amazed at such apparent impudence but holding his tongue, accompanies him (258).

Constance enters, and is surprised and delighted to meet Hastings. She quickly discovers the trick that Tony has played, and they arrange to escape to France, to be married there, once the horses are refreshed. Constance, however, must remain in her aunt's favour to get the jewels from her, and so they decide to keep Marlow in ignorance of his mistake until their own plans are completed.

Marlow returns, complaining of the landlord's and his wife's fussy attentions. Hastings introduces him to Constance, explaining that she and Kate Hardcastle just happened to be at the 'inn' to get fresh horses, having dined in the neighbourhood. Marlow is suddenly confronted with the imminent prospect of meeting his intended bride, and is covered in confusion and embarrassment. He tries to put off the meeting, but Kate herself appears in her walking dress. Hastings makes the introductions, and there follows a comically stilted and formal conversation between Marlow and Kate. Kate pretends to be as solemn as Marlow who, once deprived of Hastings's support, collapses into awkward stammering and near silence. Kate helps him through his ordeal by completing his speeches for him until Marlow makes his escape into the next room. Alone, Kate is left to reflect on Marlow's embarrassment. She finds that beneath his nervousness there are attractive qualities and that it would be worth teaching him a little self-confidence (264).

After Kate has left, Tony and Constance enter, followed by Hastings and Mrs Hardcastle. Tony is complaining that Constance will not leave him alone. She continues to flirt with him while Mrs Hardcastle tries to display her good breeding and sophistication to Hastings. He pretends to flatter her, but his flattery contains a good deal of mockery of Mrs Hardcastle's ignorance. Hastings introduces the subject of jewels and refers in conversation to Constance and Tony. Mrs Hardcastle explains that her son and niece are contracted to be married. She interrupts Constance's pretended flirtation with Tony, who is angered by her teasing and demands his fortune of his mother. They fall to squabbling, and Mrs Hardcastle leaves in a bad temper with Constance (268).

Tony and Hastings are left to themselves and Hastings invites Tony's opinion of Constance. Clearly, he cares little for her. In his eyes she is too temperamental, too unpredictable and her beauty entirely cosmetic. He much prefers the simpler charms of Bet Bouncer. Having ascertained Tony's hostility to Constance, Hastings proposes that he will relieve Tony of Constance if Tony will assist them in their elopement to France. Tony readily agrees, promising that he will also get hold of Constance's jewels for them (269).

Act III begins with Mr Hardcastle complaining about the strange behaviour of his guest. Marlow had been recommended to him by Sir

Charles as a shy and polite young man and Mr Hardcastle is at a loss to reconcile this account with what he has himself seen of Marlow. He assumes that Kate will have been as shocked by Marlow's impudent manner as himself. Kate enters, now wearing her housewife's dress, and her father asks her opinion of Marlow. As we know, each of them has seen an entirely different side of him, and when Kate expresses her surprise that such a man of the world as Marlow should be so ill-at-ease and timid, her father is completely taken aback (271). They quickly conclude that one of them must be mistaken and that whichever view of Marlow is the true one, neither can accept him. But Kate does not wish to be hasty and persuades her father to give Marlow another chance to present a more pleasing account of himself (272).

After they have left, Tony rushes in with the jewels he has taken from his mother. Hastings follows and tells Tony that he and Constance will shortly be ready to leave and that she is persisting in her attempts to acquire the jewels from her aunt without having to resort to theft. Tony tells him that there is little chance of his mother ever parting with them and hands the casket over to Hastings who leaves in some alarm at the approach of Constance and Mrs Hardcastle (273).

The two women enter, talking about the jewels. Mrs Hardcastle tries to persuade her niece that to wear her jewels would be unbecoming and casually suggests that they may in any case have gone missing. Tony, seizing the opportunity to torment his mother, whispers to her that she should indeed tell Constance they are lost and he will readily support her. Mrs Hardcastle eagerly agrees and tells Constance the jewels are mislaid and that she must be patient until they are recovered. She leaves to fetch her own cheap imitations as a substitute, just giving Tony time to reassure Constance that the jewels are safely with Hastings, before returning in a storm of fury having discovered that the jewels are genuinely missing. Tony pretends she is acting superbly, and as his mother furiously tries to tell him the truth he simply and infuriatingly agrees with her as arranged. They all leave, Mrs Hardcastle and Tony once again locked in battle (277).

Kate enters with her maid, who has just informed her of Marlow's mistaking the house for an inn. What is more, Marlow is now under the impression that Kate is the barmaid, having glimpsed her in her housewife's dress. Kate decides that she will maintain the illusion, to keep Marlow off his guard and so discover more about him before revealing her identity. The maid leaves as Marlow enters.

Marlow complains to himself about the intrusive hospitality of the innkeeper and his wife before he notices Kate. When he finally pays her some attention, he is struck by the prettiness of the 'barmaid' and immediately starts flirting with her. We now see the other side of Marlow's character as he expertly flatters her, tells her how popular he is with the ladies, and attempts to steal a kiss. Finally, he embraces her, only to be interrupted by Mr Hardcastle. Cursing his luck, Marlow hurriedly leaves (281).

Mr Hardcastle is naturally furious at his daughter's apparent untrustworthiness. He is ready to turn Marlow out of his house immediately, but Kate manages once more to calm him and to allow her an hour to prove to him that Marlow is in fact a virtuous young man of honour (281). She ends by reassuring him of her dutifulness.

Act IV begins with a brief dialogue between Hastings and Constance. She has just seen Sir Charles Marlow's letter to Mr Hardcastle which suggested that he expects to arrive shortly after his son. Hastings decides they must act urgently for he is known to Sir Charles, who would recognize him and so jeopardize the elopement. When Hastings has deposited the jewels with Marlow, they wait only for the fresh horses from Tony to make their escape. To engage Mrs Hardcastle, Constance decides to pretend that she loves Tony and then leaves (283).

Marlow enters with a servant, perplexed that Hastings should have given him a casket knowing he has no secure place to keep it. He checks with the servant that it has been given to the 'landlady' for safe keeping and, after the servant has left, muses for a moment on the attractions of the 'barmaid'. He is interrupted by Hastings, who has returned to tell Constance that their rendezvous is to be in the garden, and boasts of his imminent conquest of the 'barmaid'. Hastings, suspecting that the 'barmaid' is Kate, tries to cool his friend's ardour without revealing the 'barmaid's' identity. Marlow reassures him that he would never tamper with a woman of virtue. Hastings then asks about the security of the jewels and is horrified to learn that Marlow has inadvertently returned them to Mrs Hardcastle. He keeps his self-control, however, and leaves to prepare for departure without the jewels.

Mr Hardcastle enters, angry that his house has been turned upside-down by the behaviour of Marlow's drunken servants. He complains about their conduct to Marlow, who cannot understand why a landlord should be upset by people drinking, and calls one of his servants to prove that an abundance of liquor is being consumed. Faced by the spectacle of his guest commending the activities of his drunken servant, Mr Hardcastle can contain his wrath no longer and orders Marlow out of his house (287). Marlow angrily resists: he will not be rejected from an inn where he is a paying customer. When Mr Hardcastle expresses surprise about what Marlow's father had led him to expect of his son, the truth finally begins to dawn on Marlow.

Mr Hardcastle leaves, and when Kate enters, Marlow questions her about the house. Kate decides she must continue to deceive him and so pretends she is not a barmaid, but a poor relation of the Hardcastles who helps look after the house. Now Marlow is covered in embarrassment at his mistake and his behaviour with Mr Hardcastle. He apologizes to Kate for his forwardness when he thought her a barmaid and determines to leave. Kate now pretends to be distressed by the prospect of Marlow's departure and he finds himself moved by the young woman's mark of tenderness for him (289). He explains that, although reluctant to part from her, the differences in their upbringing and social station mean that any formal connection between them is impossible. Kate, for her part, replies by wishing she were in improved circumstances so that she should not be such a distance from him. Marlow is deeply moved by her affection for him and suggests that were it not for his obligation to his father and other people's opinion, he could choose her for his wife. As it is, he must force himself to leave. Having now seen the virtue and honour of which Marlow is capable, Kate decides she must prevent Marlow from leaving by keeping up her deception and revealing all to her father (290).

Tony and Constance enter, Tony explaining to her that the jewels have been returned to Mrs Hardcastle, who believes the servants responsible for their having gone missing. Constance is worried that if her aunt suspects her plans for elopement she will be sent away to her Aunt Pedigree where she will be a virtual prisoner. When Mrs Hardcastle enters, Tony and Constance resume their pretended courtship, acting the part of fond young lovers though also teasing one another (291). Their performance is interrupted by a servant bringing a letter for Tony, which Constance immediately recognizes as having been written by Hastings. In alarm, she tries to distract Mrs Hardcastle while the untutored Tony tries to decipher the letter. He is about to hand it to his mother when Constance snatches it from him and pretends to read the contents, inventing some nonsense about a cock-fight before trying to throw the letter away. But Tony believes her story and gives the letter to his mother who thus discovers that it is from Hastings and reveals their plans for elopement. In a towering rage, she orders Constance to prepare for her departure to Aunt Pedigree's and tells Tony to escort them (294).

As she leaves, Hastings enters to remonstrate with Tony for having revealed the letter to Mrs Hardcastle, shortly followed by Marlow, who is angry at the deception practised on him by Hastings. Constance, too, turns on Tony as the cause of all their misfortunes and the two friends draw their swords on him before returning to their own quarrel. As the moment of Constance's departure nears, the quarrel grows more heated until she manages to reconcile them and tries to comfort Hastings before hurriedly leaving. The mood of angry misery which follows her departure is broken when an idea suddenly comes to Tony. He tells Hastings to meet him in the garden in two hours' time, and rushes excitedly off stage (296).

After this moment of gloom and despondency at the end of Act IV, the final act brings about reconciliation and happiness. It begins with Hastings being informed by a servant that Mrs Hardcastle, Constance and Tony are well on their way to Aunt Pedigree's and that Sir Charles Marlow has arrived and has been laughing with Mr Hardcastle about his son's mistake. With a heavy heart, Hastings goes off to keep what he supposes will be the fruitless appointment with Tony.

Sir Charles and Mr Hardcastle enter, still amused at Marlow's misfortune and looking forward to the happy union of their children. Mr Hardcastle explains that he has himself witnessed Marlow's passion for Kate (not knowing, of course, that what he saw was Marlow's attempted conquest of a supposed barmaid) and, when Marlow enters to apologize to him once again for his behaviour, he reassures Marlow that he is forgiven and teases him about his success with his daughter (298). Once more, all is confusion as Marlow, somewhat offended, explains that his only encounter with Kate was cool and reserved. Mr

Hardcastle cannot understand why Marlow should so earnestly deny his passion for Kate. Having assured his father of his indifference to Kate, Marlow stalks out, his pride once more wounded (299). The two fathers do not know what to believe and, when Kate enters, they question her about Marlow's behaviour to her. She tells the truth: Marlow has indeed professed his love for her in the usual way (300). Sir Charles cannot believe her account of his son but Kate suggests they will see the truth for themselves if they hide away to overhear her next encounter with Marlow.

In the garden, Hastings is surprised to find Tony keeping his appointment. Covered in mud, Tony explains in a teasing riddle that he has led his mother's carriage through rough countryside in circles around the house. Mrs Hardcastle is frightened and exhausted, Constance is safe and Hastings can now escape with her easily. Hastings expresses his gratitude, and Tony reminds him of his aggressive behaviour of just a few hours ago (302). Hastings accepts the rebuke before rushing off to meet Constance while Tony detains his mother.

Mrs Hardcastle enters in a sorry state, wet, muddy and exhausted after her alarming journey through ditches and hedges. She believes they are now lost, and Tony terrifies her further with pretended glimpses of highwaymen. To his own surprise, though, a figure emerges from the gloom: his stepfather, who is taking his nightly walk. Tony tells his mother to hide: he will signal any danger by coughing. He detains his stepfather in conversation, coughing loudly all the time, until his mother, unable to bear the anxiety any longer, rushes out to plead for mercy and her precious son's life (304). Mr Hardcastle thinks his wife has gone mad; when Mrs Hardcastle recognizes him and discovers herself to be once more the victim of Tony's trick, she rushes off after her tormentor (305).

Hastings enters, urging Constance to flee with him. But Constance is exhausted, and now, in a moment of level-headed clarity, determines on the prudent course of trusting to Mr Hardcastle's compassion and justice in the hope that he will approve their bethrothal and secure her rightful inheritance from her aunt. Hastings reluctantly agrees (306).

We now return to Mr Hardcastle's house for the play's conclusion. With Mr Hardcastle and Sir Charles secretly listening, Marlow attempts to take his leave of Kate. Kate herself, still 'stooping to conquer' Marlow by pretending to be a poor relation, asks him to stay so that he might overcome his reservations about the impropriety of their connection. When Marlow insists on leaving, she accuses him of being frivolous in his attentions to her and interested only in a prosperous match. Stung, Marlow protests that her lack of prosperity is of no matter to him. He has fallen in love with her beauty and grace. Trusting that his father will approve the same qualities, he is now determined to stay. But Kate continues to pretend her disinclination, until Marlow falls to his knees as an expression of his sincerity (308). At this point his father loses his temper and emerges from hiding with Mr Hardcastle to accuse Marlow of deliberate deception. At last, the full truth is revealed to Marlow: he has fallen in love with Kate Hardcastle. He attempts to leave but is detained by Mr Hardcastle, who laughs at the mistake and tells him all is forgiven (309).

Tony enters with his mother, who consoles herself that although Hastings and Constance may have eloped, the jewels are still in her possession. Her comfort is short-lived, for the couple now enter and ask forgiveness of Mr Hardcastle for their impetuous behaviour and his permission for their betrothal. He happily concurs and then reveals to Tony that having been of age for three months, his inheritance is now his own. Tony immediately celebrates by rejecting Constance and so leaving her free to marry Hastings. Marlow congratulates his friend, who in turn invites Kate to accept Marlow. Mr Hardcastle joins the hands of his daughter and son-in-law, and, with only the petty spitefulness of Mrs Hardcastle in the background, the play ends in celebration and merriment.

Scene by Scene Analysis

PROLOGUE

The Prologue was written for Goldsmith by his friend David Garrick, one of the foremost actors and theatre-managers of his day, and spoken by Henry Woodward, a popular comic actor who was originally due to play Tony Lumpkin but turned the part down. Dressed in mourning-suit, he bemoans the sickness that has infected true comedy. If it should die, he and his fellow actor Ned Shuter (who played Mr Hardcastle) will be out of work, because true comedy would be succeeded only by an inferior kind of moralizing or sentimental play in which the actors have only to deliver comfortable moral truths in a pious manner. But a Doctor (Goldsmith himself) has devised a remedy which, should the audience accept it, will make comedy well again. The audience will judge whether the cure is effective or not by their applause, and, like a College of Physicians, they will decide whether the Doctor is genuine or a fake. For a more detailed account of the state of the theatre at this time and of Goldsmith's knowledge of medicine, see p. 9 and pp. 12–13. When you have reread these you will see how cleverly Goldsmith's talents and his play are advertised.

ACT I SCENE i

The play opens in the middle of an argument: Mrs Hardcastle is complaining to her husband about the monotonous life they lead in the country when even the dullest of their neighbours regularly visit London. Her life is tedious and isolated, punctuated by infrequent visits from the same few people and enlivened only by her husband's oft-told reminiscences: 'Ay, your times were fine times, indeed; you have been telling us of them for many a long year' (237). Whereas Mrs Hardcastle wants to be fashionable, her husband is content to lead a routine existence in rural seclusion, resisting the fashions and follies which spread out from London. In love with everything old, he teases his wife about her age (she, of course, wants to hang on to her long-passed youth): 'I love everything that's old: old friends, old times, old manners, old books, old wine; and, I believe, Dorothy (*taking her hand*), you'll own I have been pretty fond of an old wife' (237), Mr Hardcastle humorously declares.

The argument turns to Tony Lumpkin, Mrs Hardcastle's son by her first marriage, and again there is sharp disagreement between her and her husband. It is clear that Mrs Hardcastle has spoiled Tony: he was too sickly to go to school and is even now extremely delicate. Mr Hardcastle, however, regards Tony as a good-for-nothing prankster who wastes his time drinking and hunting. Tony's boisterously noisy entrance immediately marks him out as a robust young man of high spirits. His mother's attempts to detain him from another evening of high jinks at the Three Pigeons are brushed aside as he pushes her out of the way, leaving Mr Hardcastle to lament the idiotic behaviour he is forced to live with.

The one redeeming feature of his domestic life is his daughter Kate, although she too has almost fallen prey to fashionable London in her enjoyment of fine clothes. Mr Hardcastle's old-fashioned values, though, are given a moral point by Goldsmith when, looking at Kate's finery, her father declares that luxury for some means poverty for others (239). We learn, however, that Kate is willing to compromise: she dresses as she pleases in the morning but wears plain clothes to please her father in the evening.

Mr Hardcastle informs his daughter that her obedience is shortly to be tested with the arrival of Marlow, the young man he hopes will be her husband. As he lists Marlow's virtues, we see in Kate the normal reactions of a young woman: her initial guarded interest progressively turns into delight as Marlow's qualities are unfolded to her, beginning with his good sense and ending with, rather more importantly for her, his good looks. Her mounting excitement is dashed, though, by the single feature which most pleases her father but which is hardly calculated to inflame a potential lover: Marlow is 'one of the most bashful and reserved young fellows in all the world' (240). Kate shows her resolve in determining to make the best of the situation: perhaps Marlow can 'be cured of his timidity, by being taught to be proud of his wife' (241).

We are next introduced to Kate's cousin, Constance Neville, who, like Kate, is at the mercy of others' demands; in her case, it is her aunt, Mrs Hardcastle, who has fixed upon Tony as her husband in order to keep Constance's jewels in the family. So that her aunt will not suspect that she is really in love with George Hastings, Constance keeps up a pretence of affection for Tony. Noticing Kate's excited state, and learning that Marlow is her intended suitor, she supplies some curious information about him. Marlow is the close friend of Hastings and from him she has learned that while Marlow is sheepish and reserved with women of his own class, his behaviour is surprisingly different with women of a lower social status (242). Fittingly, the scene closes with the imperious calling of Mrs Hardcastle's bell summoning them both.

Notice with what skill Goldsmith has in this first scene contrived to supply us with necessary information without our being aware of his doing so. By means of natural, easy conversation, we learn the family relationships between characters, their situations and something of their personalities. The contrast between Mr and Mrs Hardcastle is immediately established. They seem to be complete opposites, but we are made to sympathize with Mr Hardcastle the more; there is genuine affection when he takes his wife's hand (237) and his sceptical view of Tony is borne out as soon as we see him. There is fairness in his treatment of Kate, for he is willing to compromise about her clothes and he will not absolutely control her choice of husband. His military obsessions are emphasized even in the details of his vocabulary, as when he complains that his servants 'want as much training as a company of recruits the first day's muster' (241). By contrast, Mrs Hardcastle is clearly tyrannical and mercenary in her dealings with Constance. Kate shows natural girlish excitement in her anticipation of Marlow, but sturdy common sense in her refusal to be discouraged when she hears of his overwhelming modesty. Even the brief impressions of Tony

Lumpkin are effective: if he is boorish and selfish with his mother, he is also, Constance tells us, 'a good-natured creature at bottom' (242). Other important details help in the development of the plot: Mrs Hardcastle's second speech (237) prepares us for the confusion of the house being mistaken for an inn, and Kate's habit of wearing a housewife's dress in the evening will later allow her to be plausibly mistaken for a serving-girl by Marlow. Finally, our curiosity is focused on Marlow; Goldsmith arouses our anticipation as we await his entrance.

ACT I SCENE ii

Tony is enjoying himself with his 'low' companions at the Three Pigeons and, as master of ceremonies, calls for silence for his song, which celebrates the superiority of drinking to learning and sobriety. The country yokels praise Tony's song as 'genteel' and cultured (which, of course, it is not). Goldsmith is here taking the opportunity to mock the genteel pretensions of his middle-class audience who had some years earlier booed a scene in his first play because it portrayed 'low' characters (see p. 13). The yokels, trying to be more cultivated than they actually are, attempt an elevated vocabulary, using words like 'concatenation' and 'maxum' (i.e. 'maxim') which they do not understand.

The merriment is interrupted by news of two London gentlemen sporting the latest fashions who are lost on their way to Mr Hardcastle's house. Tony immediately sees the chance to play a trick on his difficult stepfather. Marlow and Hastings enter. Unable to recognize Tony as a squire – and therefore of the same social station as themselves – they treat him with patronizing curtness. Tony plays the part of a subservient bumpkin, calling them 'gentlemen' and teasing them with long-winded explanations of the obvious (245) before ascertaining for himself that it is indeed his stepfather they seek. He gives an unflattering portrait of Mr Hardcastle and Kate, but in turn hears of himself as 'an awkward booby, reared up and spoiled at his mother's apron-string' (246). This makes up Tony's mind. He invents an absurdly complicated route, full of dangerous-sounding places to Mr Hardcastle's house; holds out the grim prospect of an uncomfortable night at the Three Pigeons, and so manoeuvres Marlow and Hastings into accepting his suggestion that they make their way to the 'Buck's Head'. His asides to the landlord make clear to us his plan: he will trick these two superior swells – and his stepfather into the bargain – by sending Marlow and Hastings to the Hardcastle home in the belief that it is an inn. In order to allay suspicions once the two gentlemen meet Mr Hardcastle, Tony tells them that the 'landlord' is about to give up his prosperous business and, wanting to be thought a gentleman, will show them unusual courtesy. It is with some relish, then, that Tony leads the two Londoners towards the confusion in store for them.

This scene establishes the basis of the plot which is to unfold from Tony's practical joke, as well as providing light-hearted comedy in the yokels' revelry and Tony's mischievous trickery. With amused admiration we watch Tony's clever plotting and the way in which he makes fools of the two disdainful men-about-town. Goldsmith makes Tony much the most dominant and sympathetic character in the scene. Our first impressions of various characters are confirmed: Tony is generally boisterous and popular, taking after his natural father in his love of robust country pleasures; his enjoyment of them, however, is restricted by a lack of money so he awaits his inheritance eagerly. He is quick-witted and vivid in his description of Kate as 'a tall, trapesing, trolloping, talkative maypole' (246) and the supposed route to Mr Hardcastle's home (246 and 247). Hastings tells us of Marlow's 'unaccountable reserve' in having refused to ask the way and we glimpse the sort of priggishness in Marlow's offhand treatment of Tony which is later to be developed in the encounter with Mr Hardcastle. We also find here the first instance of mistaken identity. Down from town, the two Londoners arrogantly take Tony to be another rural dimwit because of his inelegant clothing and manner. We probably feel with Tony that they are asking for their come-uppance. Above all, Goldsmith establishes a rapid comic pace and heightens the dramatic interest as we await the consequences of Tony's deviousness.

ACT II

The mistakes of the night begin. But first we see Mr Hardcastle trying to prepare his dull-witted servants for his approaching potential son-in-law, Charles Marlow. Goldsmith amusingly maintains Hardcastle's military bearing in the detailed training he tries to give the bewildered and incompetent servants, who are much more at home labouring on the farm than waiting on a genteel visitor. Again, reference is made to Mr Hardcastle's tedious habit of retelling well-worn stories of his military service, which the faithful Diggory still finds amusing (250). As Mr Hardcastle and his simple servant collapse into uncontrollable laughter we feel that while Mr Hardcastle may be exasperated with them at the moment, his relationship with his servants is essentially easy and relaxed, even if they do scatter in panic when his guests arrive. He may be something of an old stick-in-the-mud, but we see that Mr Hardcastle is fundamentally kind, good-natured and touchingly anxious to impress Marlow. It is important that Goldsmith shows him in a good light so that we always have some sympathy for him in the confusion that is to follow.

Marlow and Hastings enter, and their first remarks indicate their belief that they are now arrived at a comfortable if old-fashioned inn. Marlow is familiar with such places, and Goldsmith is able to turn their conversation easily to the topic of Marlow's shyness with one sort of woman and his forwardness with another (251). 'They are of *us*, you know', says Marlow, suggesting that females of the poorer classes are like rakish young men such as himself in their lack of modesty and scruples. Marlow explains how in the presence of refined, well-bred ladies of his own station he is paralysed by fear and embarrassment, standing in awe of them. Petrified by the prospect of formal courtship, he would much prefer an arranged marriage (252) and has only come to visit Mr Hardcastle in order to afford an easy introduction for Hastings. It seems clear that Hastings's love for Constance is genuine; he is not interested in her fortune but 'Miss Neville's person is all I ask' (253). Marlow envies his friend's ease with all sorts of women. For himself, 'I'm doomed to adore the sex, and yet to converse with the only part of it I despise' (253). He bemoans the fact that his shyness with women of his own class condemns him to consort with loose women whose attractions he might enjoy for a time but whom he fundamentally despises. Goldsmith thus re-emphasizes the contradiction in Marlow's character and prepares us for his different sorts of behaviour with Kate.

Mr Hardcastle enters to greet Marlow and is for a moment taken aback to discover *two* guests. He quickly recovers his hearty manner, only to find his attempts at hospitality rudely ignored. Marlow and Hastings discuss which fashionable clothes they should wear next morning to impress the ladies, and use a language appropriate to two rakes setting about a conquest: their metaphors of a 'campaign' and 'ammunition' completely mislead Mr Hardcastle, who thinks he can hospitably join in their conversation with his favourite war-stories. He stubbornly resists their interruptions and finally begins his tedious tale. We notice how Goldsmith captures the natural style of conversation: the repetitiousness and inconsequential asides such as '. . . you must have heard of George Brooks . . .' (254) (who, far from being famous as Mr Hardcastle supposes, seems never to have existed. Indeed, some of Goldsmith's audience might have been aware that, given its historical inaccuracies, Mr Hardcastle's story is pretty well fictitious.)

It is perhaps to our relief, as well as his own, that Marlow brusquely interrupts Mr Hardcastle with a request for punch. Disconcerted, he obliges, only to disconcert the two gentlemen in turn by insisting on joining them in a toast. To Marlow and Hastings, this appears inexplicable impudence on the part of an innkeeper, just as their impudence seems inexplicable to Mr Hardcastle. Marlow praises the punch and, making polite conversation, suggests that Mr Hardcastle must be experienced in making it, particularly at election time, when people gather at the inn to arrange the voting. (Goldsmith is referring to the corrupt electoral practices of landowners who controlled the vote in the areas they owned, known as 'pocket boroughs', and bribed the electors with drink.) When Marlow and Hastings demand the menu for supper and complain about its richness, and then ask to inspect their bedrooms, Mr Hardcastle struggles to keep his temper. As we watch the conversation lurch into increasing confusion, we enjoy the mystification of these characters who plunge deeper into an embarrassing situation which has arisen from such a simple mistake. Goldsmith handles their reactions to one another – and also their bewildered asides – with expert comic effect.

All is revealed to Hastings when Constance enters. She explains that this is the home of the Hardcastles and that Tony is no rival to Hastings. Hastings explains his plans for elopement once the horses are refreshed. Constance is determined to take her jewels and, to give themselves time, they need to keep Marlow in ignorance of his mistake, otherwise he would immediately leave the house in embarrassment. So Hastings pretends to have met Constance accidentally at the 'inn' and tells Marlow he will shortly meet Kate Hardcastle (260). Immediately, Marlow is overcome by trepidation and desperately persuades his friend not to abandon him. After Marlow's somewhat swaggering manner with Mr Hardcastle, Goldsmith now reveals the other side of his nature.

In his meeting with Kate we see Marlow at his most excruciatingly bashful. Faced with his intended bride, he collapses into stuttering embarrassment, incapable of completing a meaningful sentence, let alone sustaining a conversation. When Hastings leaves, it is left to Kate to rescue Marlow, quick-wittedly finishing his sentences for him. The spectacle of his inadequacy is hilarious but also touching – we all know what it is like to be at a loss for words. Incapable of expressing himself naturally, Marlow utters instead what he supposes he *ought* to express in such circumstances: the wooden clichés familiar to him from the novels and plays of the time. He tries to adopt a tone of suitably earnest gravity, to portray himself as a man of deep sensitivity and moral seriousness, to behave, in short, like the conventional 'man of sentiment' (263) who was then the hero of so much popular literature (see p. 13). Goldsmith is not only showing us a crucial feature of Marlow's character but also ridiculing a fashionable literary genre of his day. Marlow is paralysed by his fearfulness; Kate is amused by his bashfulness, as her waspish irony shows: 'there's something so agreeable and spirited in your manner, such life and force – pray, sir, go on' (263). Finally, he escapes into the next room, and Kate is left to laugh at him and then to ponder. Even though Marlow hardly dared look at her (this prepares us for his later failure to recognize her in her plain clothes) she has recognized 'good sense' in him, 'but then so buried in his fears, that it fatigues one more than ignorance. If I could teach him a little confidence, it would be doing somebody that I know a piece of service. But who is that somebody? – that, faith, is a question I can scarce answer' (264). Her final question is a teasing one thrown to the audience, but her speech makes clear that Kate has perceived something in Marlow's character worth further exploring.

There then follows a hilarious dialogue between Hastings and Mrs Hardcastle. Now we see in Hastings the accomplished gallantry and flattering attentiveness to women which is so painfully lacking in Marlow. Hastings uses this skill to mock Mrs Hardcastle's affectations. He exposes her real ignorance of fashionable London. All she knows of it is outdated and has been picked up from popular magazines. He first feigns astonishment that Mrs Hardcastle has not acquired her breeding in the superior areas of London. She does not realize that one of his proposed locations, Tower Wharf, was of very dubious reputation. Similarly, her list of 'where the nobility chiefly resort' is woefully inaccurate. He pretends to compliment her antique hairstyle by using a French word which Mrs Hardcastle fails to understand and employs an irony she is too vain and foolish to suspect: 'Such a head in a side-box, at the play-house, would draw as many gazers as my Lady Mayoress at a city ball' (265).

Having shown off herself, Mrs Hardcastle then tries to show off her son and niece to Hastings as a couple blissfully in love, but Tony shakes off his mother's silly attempts to treat him as a child. Thus rebuffed, she bewails Tony's supposed ingratitude: she has nursed him through incessant illnesses (of her own imagining) and tried to make a gentleman of him, and is planning to force more medicine on him next spring. She is a classic example of the indulgent mother who tries to buy affection and loyalty, and her tearfulness (an attempt to make Tony feel guilty) soon turns to spiteful anger when she fails to get her way: 'Wasn't it all for your good, viper? Wasn't it all for your good?' (267). Mrs Hardcastle may cry 'For shame, Tony. You a man, and behave so!' but she never actually treats him as a man and it is she who is the child of the two. Rather than allow him his independence, she still pampers him, when all Tony wants is his inheritance and to be left to himself: 'If I'm to have any good, let it come of itself; not to keep dinging it, dinging it into one so' (267). We surely have a good deal of sympathy with Tony, and Mrs Hardcastle, clearly a woman of volatile moods, erupts in wounded anguish, her efforts to impress Hastings as a cultivated lady doomed to failure.

Mrs Hardcastle stalks out of the room, and Hastings now discovers Tony's real attitude to Constance. Once again, we can admire the skill of Goldsmith's characterization: notice how Tony's description of Constance uses comparisons drawn from rural life which confirm him as an energetic countryman. Constance is described as a 'hare', a 'colt', a 'hog' (all suggesting how lively and animated she is) whose beauty is cosmetic compared to that of his true love, Bet Bouncer, who has the natural, healthy glow of a country girl: 'two eyes as black as sloes, and cheeks as broad and red as a pulpit cushion' (269). Having established that Tony cares little for Constance, Hastings suggests a deal. With Tony's help he will relieve him of Constance if Tony can supply fresh horses to make their escape. Tony eagerly agrees. Here is a chance to escape his mother's plans for him and to get his own back on her by stealing Constance's jewels. For Tony, who exits singing a rousing song, another mischievous scheme is afoot.

ACT III

Mr Hardcastle enters in a state of angry bewilderment. Marlow continues to treat him as a humble innkeeper, taking possession of his favourite chair and instructing him to look after his boots. Mr Hardcastle cannot understand how his old friend Sir Charles Marlow could so mislead him about his son's supposed modesty. Now he wants to know how Marlow's outrageous behaviour has affected Kate, who, he expects, will be as shocked as he is. We certainly laugh at the grotesque inappropriateness of Marlow's treatment of Mr Hardcastle, but we never find the old man entirely ridiculous because we know him to be good-natured and we sympathize with the way he struggles to keep his temper for the sake of his friendship with Sir Charles and his daughter's chances of a good marriage. But we sense that he must snap soon.

When Kate enters she is 'plainly dressed' in her housewife's garb, in fulfilment of the arrangement she has with her father. Mr Hardcastle, a little embarrassed at having introduced such an impudent monster to his daughter, tells Kate there was no need to dress so, to which Kate gives a teasing reply: 'I find such a pleasure, sir, in obeying your commands, that I take care to observe them without ever debating their propriety' (270). The suggestion that she obeys her father without question is a deliberate overstatement, for we know it is not in her nature to be so submissive. She is ironically exaggerating her dutifulness.

In the conversation that follows, Goldsmith prompts our amusement by having Kate and her father talk at cross-purposes. He, with heavy irony, refers to Marlow as 'my modest gentleman' (270) which is indeed just what Kate has seen of him and so, when they express their astonishment at his behaviour, each of them thinks they are talking about the same thing. Once that confusion is cleared up, more follows, and each reacts in equal disbelief to what the other says of Marlow. Kate has found him sheepish and impossibly reserved, Hardcastle impudent and over-familiar. If Marlow truly is what he has seemed to be to either of them, he must be rejected. But Kate is not prepared to dismiss him quite so easily, for she did manage to find something admirable in Marlow during that disastrous first interview. We may well wonder just what it was, and Kate herself cannot identify it precisely, but there is a distinctly down-to-earth practicality about her reasoning: 'I don't know – the fellow is well enough for a man. – Certainly we don't meet many such at a horse-race in the country' (272). Her father is more dogmatic: 'the first appearance' has made up his mind; but Kate persists: 'And yet there may be many good qualities under that first appearance' (272). When Mr Hardcastle suggests, rather insultingly, that Kate is trying to justify Marlow only because she finds him physically attractive, he receives a courteous rebuke: 'I hope, sir, a conversation begun with a compliment to my good sense won't end with a sneer at my understanding?' (272). Kate is an expert at maintaining outward appearances of innocent dutifulness before her father, but she knows her own mind and is not to be easily deflected from her purpose. Forced to put on appearances, she knows things are not always what they seem and this helps to explain her determination to take a second, deeper look at Marlow. Her father agrees to give Marlow a second chance but remains sceptical: 'But if young Mr Brazen [i.e. Marlow] can find the art of reconciling contradictions, he may please us both, perhaps' (272). It is Kate who will 'find the art of reconciling contradictions', by unifying the divisions between the shy and the 'brazen', or rude, in Marlow's character.

Having laid the basis for the next development in what we might call the Mr Hardcastle–Marlow–Kate plot, Goldsmith now turns our attention to the Mrs Hardcastle–Hastings–Constance plot. Tony has stolen Constance's jewels from his mother, an easy task because he regularly has to steal his own money from her and is determined that she shall not deprive Constance and Hastings of their fortune as well. Hastings tells him that Constance will continue trying to persuade her aunt to part with them freely. Tony holds out little hope: 'she'd as soon part with the only sound tooth in her head!' (273). Hastings leaves as Mrs Hardcastle and Constance enter, her aunt telling Constance that jewels are out of fashion for young ladies and that she looks pretty enough without them. We know, of course, that Mrs Hardcastle is only interested in keeping them for herself. When, trying to evade Constance's requests, she suggests that for all she knows the jewels might be missing, Tony seizes an opportunity to torment his mother. He urges her to pretend to Constance that the jewels really are missing and he will back her up. Mrs Hardcastle quickly agrees and eagerly informs Constance that the jewels are mislaid and that she must be patient until they are recovered. Given what is to come in a moment, there is a delicious irony about Mrs Hardcastle's complacency: 'You must learn resignation, my dear; for though we lose our fortune, yet we should not lose our patience. See me, how calm I am' (275). When Mrs Hardcastle leaves to fetch Constance her cheap garnets as a substitute for the jewels, Tony just has time to explain that the jewels are in Hastings's hands before his mother explodes back on to the stage: 'Zounds! how she fidgets and spits about like a catherine wheel!' (275).

Goldsmith creates wonderful comedy out of the situation: Mrs Hardcastle, trying to convince Tony (who, of course, needs no convincing) that the jewels have actually been stolen, works herself into a frenzy, ensnared by her own selfish deceitfulness. As she rages and storms, Tony provokingly compliments her on her acting performance (still pretending that they are carrying out the trick to deceive Constance) and continually cries, as arranged, 'I can bear witness to that'. Finally, as so often in the play, Mrs Hardcastle and Tony leave the stage fighting furiously.

The mood becomes calmer when Kate enters with her maid, but the dramatic pace is maintained: Tony's deception of his mother is now followed by Kate's plan to deceive Marlow. Her maid has told Kate of Marlow's mistaking the house for an inn and now tells her that Marlow has mistaken Kate for a barmaid when he briefly glimpsed her in her housewife's dress. Since he had barely looked at Kate during their first meeting, it is easy for Kate to continue his illusion as to her true identity. When she states her reasons for doing so, we again see her shrewdness: 'In the first place, I shall be seen, and that is no small advantage to a girl who brings her face to market' (277). As a girl living in rural seclusion, rarely visited by any eligible guests, she is not easily going to pass up the chance of impressing a well-bred, good-looking and rich young man. Moreover, by deceiving Marlow about her own identity, she will learn much more about his true character, particularly in view of his reticence with genteel women like herself. Good actress that she is, playing the part of barmaid and disguising her voice come easily to her, as she shows in her brief rehearsal with her maid (278).

Marlow enters, complaining about his lack of privacy: he is pestered either by Mr Hardcastle trying to finish his story or by Mrs Hardcastle's exaggerated efforts to impress. Ignoring the 'barmaid', he muses on his meeting with Kate, who, we remember, had put on the appearance of gravity. He mistakes that appearance for Kate's true nature: 'she's too grave and sentimental for me' (we know she is neither of these) and unwittingly insults her further: 'Besides from the glimpse I had of her, I think she squints' (278). He decides to return home, all the while brusquely disregarding the 'barmaid', who is attempting to catch his attention. But when he finally looks her full in the face, his tone immediately changes: the stammering, bashful Marlow who could barely utter a sentence in front of Kate is now – because he is talking to a woman he believes is his social inferior – a man of forthright directness: 'I wanted – I wanted – I vow, child, you are vastly handsome' (278). Now we see Marlow the rakish seducer of barmaids, confident and self-assured. The patter, the flattery and the impudence come with practised ease: 'Suppose I should call for a taste, just by way of trial, of the nectar of your lips . . .' (279). Within moments, he attempts to steal a kiss. We now see the other side of Marlow's nature, no longer in awe of a woman, but the expert ladykiller. Kate plays her part to perfection, leading him on and exploiting a natural sexuality that is part of her nature as it is of Marlow's. Whereas she had earlier adopted a formal manner in imitation of Marlow's, now she matches his forwardness with her own flirtatiousness. She teases Marlow by reminding him of his earlier awkwardness with 'Miss Hardcastle'. He is taken aback for a moment, but soon recovers his poise and tries to impress her by portraying himself as a man familiar and popular with women. Kate can barely control her laughter at such barefaced lying. Marlow, inflamed beyond control, clasps her in an embrace – only to find that once again he is pestered by the 'landlord', who, he assumes, is the father of the 'barmaid'. Cursing his bad luck, Marlow beats a hasty retreat.

Mr Hardcastle is outraged. Having endured Marlow's insolence, he has now found him assaulting his daughter, and his faithful, 'innocent' Kate has monstrously betrayed him. Kate tries to explain: 'Never trust me, dear papa, but he's still the modest man I first took him for, you'll be convinced of it as well as I' (281). Mr Hardcastle is determined to turn Marlow out of his house 'this very hour', but grudgingly agrees to give Kate a little time to prove her case that Marlow 'has only the faults that will pass off with time, and the virtues that will improve with age' (281). Kate finally pacifies him by once more assuming the role of gratefully dutiful daughter: 'I hope, sir, you have ever found that I considered your commands as my pride; for your kindness is such, that my duty as yet has been inclination' (282).

Act III shows Goldsmith's dramatic skill at its best. The action is fast and furious, with characters forever rushing on and off stage, devising one stratagem after another, and every speech carries the plot forward or adds a new twist to it. Yet so natural and easy is Goldsmith's dialogue that nothing appears forced or invented purely for the sake of the plot. The action grows out of the natures and personalities of his characters.

The act begins in comic confusion and ends the same way, with one character practising deception on another. Within this confusion, though, is the masterly hand of Goldsmith, showing us just enough of any situation to keep us firmly in the picture, weaving complex webs of intrigue while never straying beyond the bounds of credibility and putting before us the riddle only Kate can solve: how is she to find the art of reconciling the contradictions in Marlow's character?

In Act III we are in the very centre of the play. The act is a rapid succession of mistakes and disguises, complex knots which the rest of the play unravels. We begin with a confusion: Kate and her father talk at cross-purposes about Marlow before finding that they have received entirely contradictory impressions of him. This is followed by Tony's theft of the jewels and the trick he plays on his mother. Mrs Hardcastle attempts to deceive Constance by telling her the jewels are missing but unknown to her the intended deception in fact expresses the truth, for we know Tony has taken them. He agrees to support his mother's 'lie' about the missing jewels; then, when she rushes back on stage attempting to explain to Tony that the jewels have in truth gone missing, he blithely agrees with his mother, who thinks he is, as they arranged, only pretending to agree. In fact, he is pretending to pretend! (The confusion is further heightened, for what Tony cannot know is that even now Hastings is sending the jewels to Marlow, who will inadvertently return them to the 'landlady', as we learn at the beginning of Act IV.) Here, right at the centre of the play, is a comic situation of dizzying complexity: Tony pretends to lie and speaks the truth; Mrs Hardcastle pretends to lie and discovers it to be true, but cannot convince her son it is the truth because he pretends to think that she is lying. Watching this scene in the theatre, we pass over the brilliance of Goldsmith's contrivance in our laughter but, in reflecting on this moment, we ought to realize its significance: in a play so much concerned with disguise, deceptions and mistakes, here, at its centre, is a moment when truth and illusion become inseparable.

The illusions inexorably continue, with Marlow thinking he is seducing a barmaid and Mr Hardcastle falling into deeper confusion about Marlow and believing himself deceived by Kate, who, he thinks, has told him lies about Marlow's modesty. He is both right and wrong: wrong to believe that his daughter has lied to him about Marlow, but right to think he has been deceived by Kate. He does not know it, of course, but he has partly deceived *himself* about Kate. For when Kate twice in this act assures him that she is his passive, innocently acquiescent daughter he is all too ready to believe her. We, on the other hand, know that her worldly shrewdness and intelligence make her the only character fully in control of 'the Mistakes of a Night'. As we thus look deeper into the play, we can begin to appreciate more fully the brilliance of Goldsmith's masterly conception and design. Beneath the play's apparently simple surface lies intellectual and artistic depth.

ACT IV

This act begins the long sequence of revelations by which the characters will discover the truth about each other. Constance has learned that Marlow's father, Sir Charles, is expected shortly. Hastings is worried that his arrival will signal the discovery of their plans. He has given the jewels to Marlow and is awaiting fresh horses from Tony. Should he not see him again, Hastings will write Tony a note giving him further instructions – this prepares us for the letter which Mrs Hardcastle later reads. To buy time, Constance will engage Mrs Hardcastle by continuing her pretended affection for Tony.

When Marlow enters, we learn that Hastings's plan is already endangered, for Marlow has deposited the jewels with the 'landlady' for safekeeping. Unaware of the significance of what he has done, he blithely expresses his excitement about the 'barmaid' to Hastings: 'Such fire, such motions, such eyes, such lips ...' (284). He is bewitched by the prospect of sexual conquest, but Hastings, suspecting the 'barmaid's' true identity, is shocked: 'But how can you, Charles, go about to rob a woman of her honour?' Marlow's reply shows a distastefully dismissive attitude: 'Pshaw! pshaw! We all know the honour of a barmaid of an inn ...' (284). Here again we see that Marlow has only two attitudes to women: either they are untouchable goddesses to be admired from a distance, or they are playthings to be picked up and dropped at whim. Hastings tries to cool his friend's ardour: 'I believe the girl has virtue', and seems satisfied by Marlow's response: 'And if she has, I should be the last man in the world that would attempt to corrupt it' (284). We know enough of Marlow to believe him; he is not unscrupulous with women, just immature about them. He now proceeds to tell Hastings that he has sent the jewels to the 'landlady'. Hastings, well-bred young man that he is, manages to keep calm and quickly reconciles himself to the fact that they must leave without Constance's fortune, though there is more than a hint of bitter irony in his parting shot to Marlow: 'may you be as successful for yourself as you have been for me' (285).

Mr Hardcastle enters, once again in a fury. His house is in chaos, Marlow's servants are riotously drunk and only his regard for Marlow's father keeps him from losing his temper. Clenching his teeth, he retains his politeness to Marlow but complains about his servants' behaviour. Marlow is bemused and can only think that the 'landlord' is complaining that his servants are not drinking enough. He calls for one of them to make his point: 'I don't know what you'd have more, unless you'd have the poor devil soused in a beer-barrel' (287). Once more, we laugh at the misunderstanding, but the truth is about to dawn on Marlow. Such apparently limitless impudence is the last straw for Mr Hardcastle, who now unleashes the pent-up fervour of his wrath. In a barely controlled rage, he orders Marlow and his drunken pack out of his house. We laugh at Mr Hardcastle's mounting fury, but we also feel there is a manly dignity about his assertiveness: 'Mr Marlow, Sir; I have submitted to your insolence for more than four hours, and I see no likelihood of its coming to an end. I'm now resolved to be master here ...' (287). We laugh at the confusion of Marlow, who cannot understand why he is being turned out of an inn. Most of all, we laugh at the havoc wrought by Marlow's simple mistake of believing the house an inn. Mr Hardcastle storms out and his final words, referring to Marlow's father, leave Marlow guessing at the truth.

When Kate enters, he begins to question her, still thinking she is a barmaid. From his consternation she quickly concludes that he is beginning to see the light and decides she must tell him half the truth. She confesses that this is indeed Mr Hardcastle's house and she identifies herself as 'A poor relation appointed to keep the keys, and to see that the guests want nothing in my power to give them' (288–9). Marlow is consumed with embarrassment. His first thought is of how people will laugh at him, but he also has sufficiently good grace to see how foolishly he has behaved: 'O, confound my stupid head, I shall be laughed at over the whole town ... What a swaggering puppy must he take me for. What a silly puppy do I find myself' (289). He has made his first crucial discovery: things are not always as they appear and his generally high-handed manner has earned its come-uppance. He apologizes sincerely to Kate for treating a respectable young woman of impoverished means as a barmaid: 'My stupidity saw everything the wrong way. I mistook your assiduity for assurance, and your simplicity for allurement' (289). Ashamed and angry with himself, he resolves to quit the house immediately.

Marlow has learned a valuable lesson – but there are more to follow. Kate detains him by hinting at her affection for him and pretending to weep in sorrow at his departure. In so doing, she appeals to Marlow's finer feelings: 'By heaven, she weeps. This is the first mark of tenderness I ever had from a modest woman, and it touches me' (289). Never before has a well-born young woman shown such feeling for him and Marlow is deeply affected. His sense of honour makes it impossible that he should trifle with this girl, as he makes clear to her: 'the difference of our birth, fortune and education, make an honourable connexion [i.e. marriage] impossible' (290). This reminds us that Marlow, like Kate in a different way, is trapped. In his case it is by those conventions of his time that would make his marriage to an undistinguished country girl unseemly. When Kate laments her poverty because it puts such a gulf between them, Marlow finds his affections deepening: 'This simplicity bewitches me, so that if I stay I'm undone' (290). Suddenly, he has found a woman who in all respects but one (her social standing) would make him a perfect wife. He has accidentally fallen in love, but seemingly it must remain unfulfilled: 'were I to live for myself alone, I could easily fix my choice. But I owe too much to the opinion of the world, too much to the authority of a father . . .' (290). Deeply moved, he forces himself to leave.

It may be tempting to feel that Marlow is being spineless here and that he should rebel against the dictates of his father and of society in general. But we need to see Marlow as a product of his times, an era in which social hierarchy and class divisions were much more definite than they are now, and when ideas of personal liberty tended to take second place to the values of social stability and conformity. Certainly, Kate is pleased by what she has seen: 'I never knew half his merit till now. He shall not go, if I have power or art to detain him' (290). In descending to the role of barmaid and poor relation, she has won Marlow's heart. Having thus 'stooped to conquer', she must now 'undeceive my papa, who, perhaps, may laugh him out of his resolution'. The process towards reconciliation is under way.

For Constance and Hastings, disaster looms. The jewels are in the hands of Mrs Hardcastle, who believes them to have come her way by a mistake of the servants. The horses are ready, but Mrs Hardcastle must suspect nothing yet, so Tony and Constance put on a display of love-making. Seeing them in an embrace, Mrs Hardcastle fusses over them in delight as they exchange compliments; no doubt when Constance pats Tony's 'bold face' she pats a little too vigorously and when Tony admires her 'pretty long fingers, that she twists this way and that', he enthusiastically twists her fingers accordingly. This good-natured raillery deceives Mrs Hardcastle, though, whose joy is ecstatic; now she can safely give the jewels to Constance, who will be married to Tony tomorrow.

Her plans, however, and indeed the plans of Tony, Hastings and Constance, are shortly to come crashing down. Diggory enters with a letter for Tony which Constance recognizes as having been written by Hastings. She tries to occupy Mrs Hardcastle's attention while Tony attempts to decipher the letter, but it is beyond him. To prevent it from falling into her aunt's hands, Constance snatches it from Tony and pretends it is from Tony's chums with news of cock-fighting. She throws out a few appropriate words and phrases and, having run out of steam, tries to make Tony throw the letter away as a matter of no consequence. But for Tony, completely taken in by Constance's invention, the prospect of a cock-fight is 'of all the consequence in the world', and he eagerly hands the letter to his mother. All is lost: as she reads Hastings's instructions to Tony she falls into an apoplectic rage. Hastings, the young man who seemed the epitome of well-bred politeness, her beloved son Tony, her dutiful niece Constance, all have conspired against her. Revenge is immediate: she will escort Constance to her Aunt Pedigree where Constance will be a virtual prisoner.

As her aunt leaves to make preparations, Constance bitterly rebukes Tony, who can only defend himself by telling her that she played her part too well and completely deceived him. By a bitter irony Tony, who had so successfully deceived others, has himself been unintentionally deceived by a clever trick. Worse is to come, for now Hastings enters to show his anger at his betrayal and a moment later Marlow appears to seek revenge on the people responsible for his being 'Rendered contemptible, driven into ill manners, despised, insulted, laughed at' (294). As Constance points an accusing finger at Tony, insults are heaped on his head. In anger, Hastings and Marlow half draw their swords: Tony rises to the occasion: 'I'll fight you both one after the other', but quickly recalls that discretion is the better part of valour ' with baskets' (295). The two gentlemen contemptuously dismiss Tony and set about blaming one another for their misfortunes. Her departure now imminent, Constance interrupts them and only her real distress brings the squabbling men to their senses. She quickly reconciles them and, in this emotionally charged situation, takes her leave, trying to comfort Hastings: 'Well, my dear Hastings, if you have that esteem for me that I think, that I am sure you have, your constancy for three years will but increase the happiness of our future connexion ... Remember, constancy is the word' (296). Hastings is heartbroken and we may wonder whether, given his impetuous nature (just as Constance's name suggests her faithfulness, so Hastings's suggests his rashness) he could endure three years' waiting until Constance is of age.

Marlow rounds on Tony once more to lay the blame for such distress squarely on his shoulders: 'You see now, young gentleman, the effects of your folly. What might be amusement to you, is here disappointment, and even distress' (296). Such moralizing from Marlow is rather pompous, and not a little unfair. There follows a long moment of gloom; the play, until now so energetically exuberant, here touches a note of tragedy. The complex web of deception seems to have ensnared all the characters: Marlow seems doomed to lose the only woman he has loved; Hastings and Constance are perhaps irrevocably parted and Tony is doomed never to escape the clutches of his mother. Suddenly, Tony bursts into life: 'Ecod, I have hit it. It's here.' Without explanation, he calls for his boots, instructs Hastings to meet him in two hours' time and rushes off with the promise that they will find 'Tony Lumpkin a more good-natur'd fellow than you thought for' (296). Like Marlow and Hastings, we are baffled; like them, we must trust to Tony for success.

ACT V

This final act contains the dénouement of the play, when all the misunderstandings and complications are resolved. It opens with a servant telling Hastings that Constance, Mrs Hardcastle and Tony are well on their way, and that Sir Charles Marlow and Mr Hardcastle 'have been laughing at Mr Marlow's mistake this half-hour' (297). With little hope, Hastings goes off to keep what he supposes will be the fruitless appointment with Tony arranged at the end of the previous act.

Sir Charles and Mr Hardcastle enter in high spirits, laughing at Marlow's mistaking the house for an inn and looking forward to the marriage of Kate and Marlow, Mr Hardcastle assuring his friend of their children's mutual affection. Marlow enters to ask forgiveness once more from Mr Hardcastle for his impudent behaviour. Good-natured fellow that he is, Mr Hardcastle brushes the matter aside and teases Marlow about the young man's successful wooing of Kate. Marlow, of course, is once again at a loss; his meeting with Kate occasioned only 'the most profound respect on my side, and the most distant reserve on hers' (298). Mr Hardcastle assures him that he need not be embarrassed about what has passed between him and Kate (the last he saw of them was Marlow passionately embracing his daughter). They are both men of the world, he says, and 'girls like to be played with, and rumpled a little too, sometimes' (298). Marlow hotly denies any such behaviour and once more Mr Hardcastle is astonished by what appears to be the most brazen lying: 'This fellow's formal modest impudence is beyond bearing' (299). For his part, Marlow too is confused by the suggestions that he has shamelessly flirted with Kate and in some anger takes his leave: 'I hope you'll exact no further proofs of my duty, nor prevent me from leaving a house in which I suffer so many mortifications' (299).

As Marlow, his pride again sorely wounded, leaves the stage, we find once more a character caught in an ironic situation (that is, a situation which we understand more fully than the character at its centre). Marlow, whose timidity prevents him from even talking to young ladies of rank, has just been teased about his bold wooing of a squire's daughter. As far as he knows, nothing could be further from the truth and he knows himself to be the last man on earth to attempt such a thing. Having suffered so many other indignities in Mr Hardcastle's house, the suggestion that he, with his reputation for modesty, has been so forward with a respectable young woman is the last straw. And yet, of course, although Marlow does not know it, this is precisely what has occurred. We might at this point recall something Marlow said earlier in the play when he was explaining his difficulty with women to Hastings: 'An impudent fellow may counterfeit modesty, but I'll be hanged if a modest man can ever counterfeit impudence' (252). How wrong he was! Modest he may be, but all through the play he has appeared intolerably impudent to Mr Hardcastle and now he is being congratulated on what in his own eyes is the greatest impudence of all. It is true that Marlow has not deliberately set out to 'counterfeit impudence', to assume a forward manner. But what the play has shown is that the way we appear to others can be very different from the way we appear to ourselves.

After Marlow's vigorous denial, Mr Hardcastle and Sir Charles are at a loss to know what to believe and when Kate enters she is closely questioned about Marlow's behaviour. She tells them the truth, that Marlow has indeed ardently professed his love for her. She shows a clear-sighted shrewdness in her estimation of his behaviour: 'Said some civil things of my face, talked much of his want of merit, and the greatness of mine; mentioned his heart, gave a short tragedy speech, and ended with pretended rapture' (300). Kate is not a girl to be taken in by the conventional expressions of love alone and we know that she is able to see through appearances, as she has had to do in order to detect Marlow's real merit. Sir Charles cannot believe that Kate's description could possibly apply to his shy and inexperienced son, so Kate proposes that if he and her father hide themselves behind a screen, in half an hour's time 'you shall hear him declare his passion to me in person' (300).

The scene changes to the garden, where Hastings is forlornly awaiting Tony. To his surprise, Tony arrives and answers his questions with teasing riddles before explaining that he has driven his mother and Constance round and round the surrounding countryside on a perilous journey circling the house (301–2). His mother is now exhausted and terrified by the 'accidents' Tony has led her into so that Hastings should have no difficulty making his escape with Constance. When Hastings is duly trying to thank him, Tony rebukes him for having earlier threatened him: 'Just now, it was all idiot, cub, and run me through the guts. Damn your way of fighting, I say. After we take a knock in this part of the country, we kiss and be friends' (302). Here we are reminded of something of the difference between the manners of the town and of the country. The grateful Hastings had not long ago drawn his sword on Tony with dashing flamboyance, albeit in the heat of the moment. Tony is complaining not only about the insults he had received, but also pointing out to Hastings that the impulsive, swashbuckling code of conduct practised by fashionable young men of London like Hastings compares badly with the slower, more generous ways of the country. The well-bred London gentleman has to bow to the simple countryman whose sense of justice is wiser than his own; Hastings honourably admits that 'The rebuke is just' (302).

Hastings rushes off to help Constance, as Mrs Hardcastle, bemused, battered and bruised, limps on stage. Tony torments her further with pretended glimpses of highwaymen, only to find that there is indeed a figure walking towards them: Mr Hardcastle on his nightly stroll. Tony tells his mother it is a highwayman armed to the teeth and sends her away to hide. When Mr Hardcastle, surprised to see Tony, angrily demands the truth from him, Tony continues to frighten his mother by pretending he is in mortal danger. Finally unable to contain herself, Mrs Hardcastle rushes out of hiding in fear for her precious son's safety. This is perhaps her most sympathetic moment in the play, for although her terror is comical, there is a touching courage in her desperate attempts to save her son. Mr Hardcastle is confronted by the spectacle of his wife on her knees begging mercy of him and this hilarious situation ends with Mr Hardcastle explaining to her that she has been tricked by Tony, who once more has to bear his mother's wrath. His parting words, however, express to his mother an unpalatable truth: 'Ecod, mother, all the parish says you have spoiled me, and so you may take the fruits on't' (305).

For Hastings and Constance, the way is now clear to elope. But Constance, exhausted by the journey, now sees things in a different light. 'Prudence once more comes to my relief, and I will obey its dictates. In the moment of passion, fortune may be despised, but it ever produces a lasting repentance' (305). Again, we see how level-headed intelligence belongs to the two young women in the play; Constance has a practical appreciation of the value of money, just as Kate was earlier unwilling to let the chance of attracting a well-to-do gentleman slip by. She must throw herself on Mr Hardcastle's mercy, and Hastings can only reluctantly agree.

As the scene changes back to Mr Hardcastle's house, we begin the final unravelling of the plot's last strand. After Sir Charles has left to fetch Mr Hardcastle, Marlow enters to take his final leave of Kate, who he still believes to be the poor relation of the family. He again falls under her spell and finds it increasingly difficult to part from her: 'The disparity of education and fortune, the anger of a parent, and the contempt of my equals, begin to lose their weight . . .' (306). What Kate now has to do is to help Marlow overcome the barriers of convention, to force him to realize that if his love for her is genuine it cannot be so easily compromised by the world's opinion. She pretends to be hurt by his consciousness of her social inferiority: 'I must have only the mockery of your addresses, while all your serious aims are fixed on fortune' (307). Now, in the hearing of his father and Mr Hardcastle, Marlow expresses his love for Kate: 'But every moment that I converse with you, steals in some new grace, heightens the picture, and gives it stronger expression. What at first seemed rustic plainness, now appears refined simplicity. What seemed forward assurance, now strikes me as the result of courageous innocence, and conscious virtue . . . I am now determined to stay, madam, and I have too good an opinion of my father's discernment, when he sees you, to doubt his approbation' (307). But Kate is not ready to let him off the hook just yet and continues to test the strength of his affection. Finally, the young man who could treat women only with remote subservience or playful flirtatiousness falls on his knees before the woman who has led him into love.

A moment later, though, he is in amazement, accused of deception by his father and Mr Hardcastle (who of course do not know of his ignorance of Kate's true identity) and he discovers that he has declared his love to none other than the cold and distant Kate Hardcastle whom he had so feared to meet. In confusion, he turns to go, but is held back by the now enlightened and forgiving Mr Hardcastle: 'I see it was all a mistake, and I am rejoiced to find it . . . We'll all forgive you. Take courage, man' (309). As Mrs Hardcastle and Tony enter, Marlow is taken to the back of the stage to be teased out of his consternation by Kate.

It only remains for Constance and Hastings to win the approval of Mr Hardcastle. Sir Charles commends the match, describing Hastings as 'As worthy a fellow as lives, and the girl could not have made a more prudent choice' (309). When they enter, Mr Hardcastle grants his permission readily after Hastings's dignified apology and Constance's explanation of how she had been 'obliged to stoop to dissimulation to avoid oppression' (310). But one last surprise is in store. Mr Hardcastle invites Tony formally to refuse Constance and explains that having kept his true age a secret in an attempt to improve Tony he now sees how his wife 'turns it to a wrong use' and reveals to him that 'you have been of age these three months' (310). In a brief parody of the marriage ceremony, Tony delightedly renounces Constance, thus releasing her to Hastings, and proudly declares, 'Tony Lumpkin is his own man again!' (310). It is then left to Hastings to conjoin Marlow and Kate: 'Come, madam, you are now driven to the very last scene of all your contrivances. I know you like him, I'm sure he loves you, and you must and shall have him' (311). With only the dissenting voice of Mrs Hardcastle in the background, we find the two couples finally united and Tony liberated from his mother to pursue his independence. 'The Mistakes of a Night' are crowned by reconciliation, celebration, and the promise of marriage and merriment in the morning.

EPILOGUE

The epilogue is spoken by the actress playing Kate Hardcastle. Having gained a husband by being mistaken for a barmaid, she will keep that character in order to win the audience's approval. A woman's life is like a play: the first 'act' shows her young and innocent; the second 'Th' unblushing barmaid of a country inn', now enjoying her feminine charms. By the third 'act' the country girl has become the toast of the town; in the fourth, she has married well and affects an elegant, sophisticated lifestyle, but as she grows older so she loses 'the power to kill'. The final 'act' belongs to the actress who now claims her applause from the audience.

Characters

MR HARDCASTLE

Poor Mr Hardcastle! With a silly, vain, nagging wife and an idle prankster for a stepson, it is no wonder he yearns for the past and sees the modern age as infected by folly and corruption: 'But is not the whole age in a combination to drive sense and discretion out of doors?' (239). Only his daughter Kate has escaped the full effect of the modern disease, albeit narrowly, for even she dresses with fashionable extravagance in the morning: 'What a quantity of superfluous silk hast thou got about thee, girl! I could never teach the fools of this age, that the indigent world could be clothed out of the trimmings of the vain' (239). But he has a good relationship with Kate; he will not force a husband she does not like on her, he gives her the opportunity to change his mind about Marlow and his trust in her is absolute. He has a strict sense of what is right and what is wrong, and it is everything old that is best: 'I love everything that's old: old friends, old times, old manners, old books, old wine; and, I believe, Dorothy (*taking her hand*), you'll own I have been pretty fond of an old wife' (237). Not surprisingly, Mrs Hardcastle takes offence at this doubtful compliment! She complains, loudly but in vain, about the life of unnatural seclusion they lead, never visiting London, and about how boring and repetitive Mr Hardcastle's habitual nostalgia is: 'Ay, your times were fine times, indeed; you have been telling us of them for many a long year' (237).

Mr Hardcastle is no fool, though. He knows what harm his wife's spoiling has done to Tony, 'a mere composition of tricks and mischief!' (237) and recognizes that she is only getting her just deserts when Tony torments her: 'Ay, there goes a pair that only spoil each other' (239). His impatience with Tony has to counterbalance his wife's doting indulgence of the young man and there is a sharp-tongued wit in his sarcasm (238).

Mrs Hardcastle. . . . Anybody that looks in his face may see he's consumptive.
Hardcastle. Ay, if growing too fat be one of the symptoms.
Mrs Hardcastle. He coughs sometimes.
Hardcastle. Yes, when his liquor goes the wrong way.
Mrs Hardcastle. I'm actually afraid of his lungs.
Hardcastle. And truly, so am I; for he sometimes whoops like a speaking-
    trumpet . . .

However, after Tony himself has rounded on his mother for having spoiled him and tells her she has earned the consequences, Mr Hard-castle has the maturity of judgement to see some sense in him: 'There's morality, however, in his reply' (305).

In his younger days, Mr Hardcastle was a soldier and claims to have fought under Marlborough, the most famous commander of the age. Just as he is obsessed with the past, so he loves to relive his glorious campaigns, the details of which owe much to his invention. He tries to prepare his servants for his impending guest, Marlow, with military precision and, although he is a little imperious and irritable, the familiarity with which he and the servants treat each other suggests a basic human kindness. They are not frightened of him and are still willing to laugh at his oft-repeated jokes (250). With Marlow and Hastings his manners are hospitable with an old-fashioned attentive-ness: 'It's not my way, you see, to receive my friends with my back to the fire. I like to give them a hearty reception in the old style at my gate' (253). Even when they rudely ignore him (supposing him the innkeeper), he flutters around them, trying to force upon them his wartime reminiscences, having mistaken their military metaphors (they are in reality talking about 'opening the campaign' in the attempted conquest of females) as an invitation to entertain them. He is surprised by requests for punch, amazed at their impudent remarks about the menu and astonished at being ordered around his own home. But still he keeps his temper in front of them, only expressing outrage privately to Kate about Marlow's reputed modesty: 'He spoke to me as if he knew me all his life before; asked twenty questions, and never waited for an answer; interrupted my best remarks with some silly pun, and when I was in my best story of the Duke of Marlborough and Prince Eugene, he asked if I had not a good hand at making punch. Yes, Kate, he asked your father if he was a maker of punch!' (271). Kate has seen a very different side of Marlow, and Mr Hardcastle shows his faith in her and a commendable open-mindedness in allowing her to prove her case: 'But if young Mr Brazen can find the art of reconciling contradictions, he may please us both, perhaps' (272). Even when he discovers Marlow attempting to seduce his daughter, he keeps his self-control, which suggests the completeness of his trust in Kate. His patience snaps when Marlow's drunken servants grow unmannerly and there is a manly dignity in the bitter irony of his mounting rage: 'Pray sir, (*bantering*) as you take the house, what think you of taking the rest of the furniture? There's a pair of silver candlesticks, and there's a firescreen, and here's a pair of brazen-nosed bellows, perhaps you may take a fancy to them?' (287–8).

By the time we see Mr Hardcastle again, he has discovered Marlow's mistake and is able to enjoy the misunderstanding with his old friend Sir Charles; he is too mellow and well-tempered to bear a grudge. His forgiveness of Marlow is genuine, as are his hopes of a happy marriage. But he is perplexed by Marlow's protestation of formal reserve in his dealings with Kate; once more, he must trust to Kate to reveal the truth. When he sees Marlow treating Kate with more passion than he has admitted to, he is brisk in his condemnation of Marlow, not for his forwardness, but for his apparent deceitfulness: 'It means that you can say and unsay things at pleasure. That you can address a lady in private, and deny it in public; that you have one story for us, and another for my daughter!' (308). But his anger immediately subsides when he realizes how Marlow's behaviour is due to an honest mistake and he then brings about the final reconciliations between Marlow and Kate and Hastings and Constance. He even shows affection for Tony in revealing the truth of his age and granting him his inheritance – and his freedom from Mrs Hardcastle – as he rounds off the play in a spirit of jovial celebration.

In many ways, Mr Hardcastle is a typical father-figure in the plays of Goldsmith's day, a relic from a bygone era – 'a piece of antiquity' Mrs Hardcastle calls him – surviving into an age he does not understand, gulled by the younger generation who must deceive him in order to live their own lives in their own way. But Goldsmith makes him a sympathetic and admirable character; his sense of decency and honour, his fairness to his daughter, his tolerance of his wife and stepson, his good-humoured, forgiving nature are all values which make him an individual personality rather than a character-type and which surely call for our approval.

MRS HARDCASTLE

Mrs Hardcastle is the least sympathetic character in the play; she comes the nearest to being the villain of the piece. She early appears as silly and vain, ridiculously desperate to seem fashionable and sophisticated. She is impatient with Mr Hardcastle, her second husband, and is thoroughly bored (perhaps understandably) by his old-fashioned habits and rural seclusion. Their squabble about Tony Lumpkin, her son by her previous marriage, is undoubtedly one of many. Having spoiled and over-protected him, she now has to make excuses for his idleness. He has had no schooling because in her eyes he has always been too sickly. She is obviously proudest of his future inheritance of £1,500 a year, and this is the first indication of her mercenary nature. Her behaviour with Tony when we first see them together early in Act I is typical; her attempts to detain him are plaintively wheedling, and finally childishly petulant. Her disapproval of Tony's drinking companions also confirms her as a conventional snob. She is easily impressed by the smooth cosmopolitan manners of Hastings, whose dubious compliments in fact ridicule her affectations and expose her as a vain simpleton.

Her self-centredness is at its most monstrous when it comes to money. She has sole management of Constance's fortune and will not allow her to wear her jewels; she at first pretends they are worthless (274) and have gone missing but explodes in passionate fury when she discovers they have actually been stolen (by Tony, who has given them to Hastings). By accident, the jewels are returned to Mrs Hardcastle, and she can pursue her plan to keep the fortune safely in the family by arranging a marriage between Tony and Constance. She parades them together before Hastings, Constance's real love, until as usual, she allows herself to be provoked by Tony and relapses into petty squabbling and self-pity (267). Before too long, though, she is all smiles when she thinks she discovers Tony and Constance 'fondling together' and threatens them with marriage the next day. But her plans are shattered when she reads Hastings's letter to Tony asking for fresh horses to speed his elopement with Constance (293). Her wrath is tyrannical and she determines upon escorting Constance (with Tony as guard) to her Aunt Pedigree, who 'will keep you secure' (294).

Her distress and degradation are thoroughly deserved as Tony leads her a merry dance through the swamps and ditches of the surrounding countryside. But it is at this time that she is seen at her most admirable; there is a touching courage in her willingness to sacrifice herself for her beloved Tony to the 'highwayman' (in reality her husband). This soon turns to mortified anger, though, in the final scene, when Tony, now revealed to be of age, formally renounces Constance, who is united with Hastings. Mrs Hardcastle's is the only sour voice in the general good will at the play's end.

Mrs Hardcastle's behaviour veers between childish rage and cold-hearted calculation. She is a mixture of selfishness and simple gullibility – in other words, she is easily tricked. Having indulged her son's whims she earns only his rebuke: 'Ecod, mother, all the parish says you have spoiled me, and so you may take the fruits on't' (305). She is not at all likeable, but by the end of the play she has been made a figure of fun, too ridiculous to deserve anything more severe than our pity for her foolishness.

TONY LUMPKIN

Tony is the most forceful character in the play, and in some ways the most interesting. He has a reckless energy; it is his plots, tricks and intrigues which drive the play along and each new difficulty he gets into and escapes from adds a new twist to the plot.

His name seems to tell us a good deal about him: 'Tony' was a slang name for a fool or simpleton and 'Lumpkin' is suggestive of dull-wittedness. But even in this we are deceived about him, for we will find that Tony is none of these. Certainly, he is a type of country bumpkin, lacking the refined manners of the city. In the opening scene we learn that he is a prankster (who drives his stepfather, Mr Hardcastle, to distraction) and is spoiled by a doting mother. He has received no formal education because his mother thought him too sickly (his healthy trumpeting even before he comes on stage puts the lie to that) and is to inherit £1,500 per annum when he is of age. Our first view of him is as a young man who is intent only on pursuing his own pleasure at the Three Pigeons and treats his mother rather boorishly. She intends him to marry his cousin Constance to keep her money in the family and although it is plain Tony cares little for Constance his mother will not accept this obvious truth. Nevertheless, it is on this topic that we hear the first good of him (242):

Miss Hardcastle. My good brother holds out stoutly. I could almost love him for hating you so.
Miss Neville. It is a good-natured creature at bottom, and I'm sure would wish to see me married to anybody but himself.

Whatever Tony's faults, a mercenary or money-loving nature is not one of them.

Indeed, the second scene shows him as popular and generous with his friends (remember, too, that Tony occupies a higher social status than they, but, unlike his mother, he has no trace of snobbery). It seems he takes after his father in his zest for healthy, energetic pursuits. When he hears of the two London swells lost on their journey to Mr Hardcastle, he immediately sees an opportunity to get his own back on his stepfather. Their patronizing attitude annoys him, particularly when they unwittingly refer to him by reputation as 'an awkward booby, reared up and spoiled at his mother's apron-string' (246). Vengeance is easy: he directs them to an 'inn' which is actually his own home, warning them (and thus allaying their suspicions) that they will find the 'landlord' unusual in his attempts to be a gentleman.

By the time we see Tony again, Hastings and Constance have discovered his trick but have decided to keep Marlow in ignorance so as to give themselves time to arrange their elopement. It is clear that Tony is desperate to escape his mother's clutches and her plans of marrying him to Constance, and his violent outbursts in front of

Hastings express his exasperation: 'If I'm a man, let me have my fortin. Ecod! I'll not be made a fool of no longer ... I wish you'd let me and my good alone, then. Snubbing this way when I'm in spirits. If I'm to have any good, let it come of itself; not to keep dinging it, dinging it into one so' (267). The way is clear for Tony to plot his next intrigue with Hastings whereby Hastings will relieve Tony of Constance, leaving him free to pursue the fleshier charms of one Bet Bouncer, in return for Tony's help in securing Constance's jewels and horses. Soon, there is another opportunity for Tony to exercise his native cunning. Having stolen Constance's jewels, he urges his mother to tell Constance they are missing, assuring her that he will support her story through thick and thin. When Mrs Hardcastle discovers that they are actually missing, as Tony well knows, Tony twists the knife by carrying on the pretence. His repetition of 'I can bear witness to that' and deliberate misunderstanding of his mother's genuine anguish is a comic masterpiece, a triumph of his wit over her greed. There is a satisfying poetic justice to it all.

But, by a delicious irony, Tony too is tricked by a piece of deception he takes to be truth. When Constance 'reads' the contents of Hastings's letter to Tony, Tony believes her invention 'about cocks, and fighting' and hands it to his mother as a matter of urgent interest. All is revealed: Mrs Hardcastle rages, Constance, Hastings and Marlow turn on him, and poor Tony finds that he is caught in the web of his own weaving. He may threaten to fight the two gentlemen 'one after the other', but this alone will not atone for the real harm and pain he has caused: 'You see now, young gentleman, the effects of your folly. What might be amusement to you, is here disappointment, and even distress' (296). At this moment of crisis, Tony's wit and inventiveness do not desert him: one more daring deception will restore the situation.

Tony milks his final trick for all it is worth. Having driven his exhausted mother through hedges and ditches in circles, he returns to announce his triumph to Hastings in taunting riddles and verbal quips (301):

Tony. Left them? Why, where should I leave them, but where I found them?
Hastings. This is a riddle.

Tony. Riddle me this, then. What's that goes round the house, and round the
   house, and never touches the house?
Hastings. I'm still astray.
Tony. Why, that's it, mon. I have led them astray.

Then he torments his mother with pretended glimpses of robbers and
highwaymen, only to find that there is indeed a figure approaching: Mr
Hardcastle, who is naturally bemused to find his wife on her knees
begging for mercy. Having led her a merry dance, Tony finally delivers
a telling home truth to his mother: 'Ecod, mother, all the parish says
you have spoiled me, and so you may take the fruits on't' (305).
His reward is his liberty. Granted his inheritance and released from
Constance, 'Tony Lumpkin is his own man again!' (310).
   Like other characters in the play, Tony is a man who has to escape
from his circumstances. Condemned by his mother to remain a child,
wrongly deprived of independent means (she lies to him about his age),
resorting to theft in order to lead some life of his own ('An honest man
may rob himself of his own at any time' (273)), Tony has been forced
to rely on his own wits: he needs no formal education. His childish
pranks and drinking bouts are the only outlets for his high spirits. He
may not be sophisticated, but he is shrewd (he knows perfectly well he
has been spoiled), clever and fundamentally honest and honourable (his
rebuke to Hastings is justified: 'Damn your way of fighting, I say. After
we take a knock in this part of the country, we kiss and be friends'
(302).) If he is sometimes idiotic, it is because he is so often treated as
an idiot. His most obvious quality is his untiring verve and energy, a
vigour that colours his language, from his explosive curses to his
description of Constance ('as many tricks as a hare in a thicket, or a colt
the first day's breaking') and the vivid Bet Bouncer: 'Ecod, she has two
eyes as black as sloes, and cheeks as broad and red as a pulpit cushion'
(268–9). We are irresistibly drawn to Tony more than to any other
character, with the exception of Kate: he has the mental agility and
instinctive cunning to seize upon and make the best of any opportunity
that comes his way. Like the characters in the play, we discover Tony
to be 'a more good-natured fellow' than was bargained for.

KATE HARDCASTLE

Kate is a likeable girl of youthful high spirits and a good deal of natural charm. She shares her stepmother's interest in fashion, though not to such an absurd extent; she is allowed to dress as she pleases in the morning and she enjoys reading the popular 'sentimental' novels, which were meant to leave the reader in floods of tears (268). But she is also a dutiful daughter to her father (though not as compliant as he believes), wearing her housewife's dress in the evening to please him and agreeing to meet the man he has chosen as her husband.

Kate's situation is typical of that of a country girl in the eighteenth century, when marriages were arranged to unite families sharing common interests and the individuals involved, particularly the girl, had little choice in the matter (although her father tells Kate: 'Depend upon it, child, I never will control your choice' (240)). So, although a little taken aback at the imminence of her meeting with Marlow, Kate merely suggests that 'our meeting will be so formal, and so like a thing of business, that I shall find no room for friendship or esteem' (240). But her reservations are quickly overcome as her father describes Marlow as young, generous and brave, and very handsome: 'My dear papa, say no more (*kissing his hand*). He's mine, I'll have him' (240). In a moment, though, her hopes are dashed; her father might gladly declare Marlow to be 'one of the most bashful and reserved young fellows in all the world', but Kate is sufficiently practical to know 'A reserved lover, it is said, always makes a suspicious husband' (240) and she naturally wants a companion whose temperament matches her own liveliness. On the other hand, she must also recognize that catches like Marlow are rare for 'a girl who brings her face to market' (277). So she must make the best of the situation and 'trust to occurrences for success' (242). We quickly warm to her mixture of gaiety and level-headedness: 'Well, if he refuses, instead of breaking my heart at his indifference, I'll only break my glass for its flattery, set my cap to some newer fashion, and look out for some less difficult admirer' (240–41).

Her first interview with the stammering and sheepish Marlow shows her shrewd intelligence in drawing him out and sustaining his flagging conversation as she quick-wittedly completes his sentences for him. Hers is an inventive performance, particularly as we know that the morally serious tone she adopts and the sombre convictions she expresses are absurdly at odds with what we know to be her true nature. It is to her credit that she is generous and perceptive enough to see that 'He has good sense, but then so buried in his fears, that it fatigues one more than ignorance' (264).

When Kate and her father discuss Marlow she shows her independence of mind and confidence in her own judgement, persuading him that they ought 'to make further discoveries'. She robustly answers her father's scepticism and more than stands up for herself: 'I hope, sir, a conversation begun with a compliment to my good sense won't end with a sneer at my understanding?' (272). A country girl she may be, but she is no fool, particularly when it comes to judging Marlow's ardour when he believes her to be a poor relation of the Hardcastles (300):

Sir Charles. And how did he behave, madam?
Miss Hardcastle. As most professed admirers do. Said some civil things of my face, talked much of his want of merit, and the greatness of mine; mentioned his heart, gave a short tragedy speech, and ended with pretended rapture.

This shrewd irony ridicules not only Marlow's behaviour, but also the conventional rituals of courtship popular in the literature of that time. But she has found much to like and admire in Marlow, whom she has successfully deceived so that she may see him more at ease, and is determinedly persuasive in convincing her father and Sir Charles to hide so that she may reveal his true nature to them. In that final interview, she has to test the authenticity of Marlow's love for her and examine his real motives before the true situation is revealed to him; she does so in a language that sincerely conveys true depth of feeling.

Like her cousin Constance, Kate is a girl who knows what she wants and uses all her abilities to get it. We need to bear in mind that Kate lives in difficult circumstances. Her father imposes a dull routine on his household and expects her obedience; she has little in common with her stepmother and, living in rural seclusion, she may never meet a man whose charm and intelligence can match her own. In the end, Kate wins a husband satisfactory not only to her father but to herself as well. She achieves her own desires, though in a way which carefully avoids open rebellion. She allows her father to believe she is as innocent as she sometimes makes herself appear, seeming ever eager to obey his commands.

Where Tony's tricks owe something to malice and retribution, hers are restorative, beneficent. There is nothing selfish, mercenary or untrustworthy about her; her father declares that he would stake his happiness upon her veracity (299). She is an honest, good-hearted girl who is forced to 'stoop' to deception in order to win true happiness for herself and others. She fully deserves Marlow's praise of her 'refined simplicity . . . courageous innocence and conscious virtue' (307). She is quick-witted in turning Tony Lumpkin's trick on Marlow to her own advantage so that she can discover his virtues for herself; shrewd, too, in seeing in Marlow a capacity to become a true lover rather than a seducer of barmaids; inventive in her disguise and attractive in her wit. She is the true heroine of the play, for it is she who, by her good sense and strength of personality, manages to 'find the art of reconciling contradictions'. In reconciling the extremes of Marlow's nature, she discovers a man whose honour and affection make him worthy of her.

CONSTANCE NEVILLE

In love with George Hastings, Constance is beset by difficulties. Although her deceased father had approved their marriage, she is now the ward of Mrs Hardcastle, who guards her jewels with jealous possessiveness and intends to keep them in the family by marrying Constance to her son Tony Lumpkin. So Constance has to pretend to love Tony in the hope that Mrs Hardcastle will let her wear the jewels, at which point she plans to elope with Hastings. In reality, Tony and Constance do not care for each other, but both are good actors and so are able to deceive Mrs Hardcastle for as long as necessary.

Constance resembles her cousin Kate in her quick-wittedness and liveliness: Tony describes her as having 'as many tricks as a hare in a thicket, or a colt the first day's breaking . . . when she's with her playmates, she's as loud as a hog in a gate' (268). She shows admirable determination, patience and good humour in coping with Mrs Hardcastle. She leads Hastings in the plan to keep the truth from Marlow and shows her shrewdness in trying to help Marlow overcome his embarrassment at his impending introduction to Kate: 'Your ceremony will displease her. The disorder of your dress will shew the ardour of your impatience' (261). But she is trapped by her own inventiveness when she makes up the contents of Hastings's letter to Tony and then has to suffer the dreadful consequences of Mrs Hardcastle's wrath. Her natural good spirits and optimism quickly surface, though, and she pacifies Marlow and Hastings while characteristically trying to make the best of the situation: 'Well, my dear Hastings, if you have that esteem for me that I think, that I am sure you have, your constancy for three years will but increase the happiness of our future connexion' (296).

It is when success is within her grasp that Constance's sense of duty comes to the fore: 'Prudence once more comes to my relief, and I will obey its dictates. In the moment of passion, fortune may be despised, but it ever produces a lasting repentance' (305). There is real courage in her determination to explain all to Mr Hardcastle and trust to his compassion. When she reveals how she has 'been obliged to stoop to dissimulation to avoid oppression' (310), she is not only describing how she has had to trick and deceive in order to win happiness but also expressing how degrading and unworthy such duplicity has been. Her natural sense of right and wrong means that she is sufficiently perceptive and just to see good in other people – early in the play she describes Tony as 'a good-natured creature at bottom' (242). When at last she is free of Mrs Hardcastle's designs and able to marry Hastings, we feel that her constancy (she is appropriately named by Goldsmith) is justly rewarded.

YOUNG MARLOW

The son of Sir Charles Marlow, an old friend of Mr Hardcastle, Marlow is helping his friend Hastings to meet the Hardcastle family and so renew his courtship with Constance. At the same time, Marlow is seen by both his father and by Mr Hardcastle as a suitor to Kate; Mr Hardcastle tells his daughter of Marlow's intelligence, generosity, good looks and, 'to crown all, Kate, he's one of the most bashful and reserved young fellows in all the world' (240). Kate is disappointed, but determines upon surmounting this obstacle: 'Yet can't he be cured of his timidity, by being taught to be proud of his wife?' (241). She is even more intrigued when Constance, knowing of Marlow through Hastings, tells her of another side to Marlow: 'He's a very singular character, I assure you. Among women of reputation he is the modestest man alive; but his acquaintance give him a very different character among creatures of another stamp: you understand me' (242).

In the very first scene of the play, then, Marlow is established as a character of two extremes: reserved and bashful with women of his own class but a practised seducer of girls of a lower status. His shyness is again stressed by Hastings when we first see the two friends together: they are lost because of 'that unaccountable reserve of yours that would not let us inquire more frequently on the way' (245). Marlow's reply is interesting: 'I own, Hastings, I am unwilling to lay myself under an obligation to everyone I meet, and often stand the chance of an unmannerly answer' (245). Does this express shyness, or a sense of priggish, disdainful superiority? Perhaps we take some pleasure in Tony Lumpkin's making fools of the London sophisticates by sending them off to the Hardcastle house under the impression that it is an inn.

Marlow's behaviour with Mr Hardcastle is, of course, hilariously inappropriate: he treats as a servant a man who is destined to be his father-in-law. Believing him the innkeeper, Marlow interrupts his stories, orders him to make punch, mocks his food and insists on inspecting the accommodation, all the while growing more impatient: 'A very troublesome fellow this, as ever I met with' (258). The joke is on Marlow, of course, in mistaking a house for an inn and its occupants for servants, but we might ask ourselves whether we do not find his patronizing and high-handed attitude with the 'innkeeper' embarrassing as well as amusing. And do we not enjoy his discomfiture when he is about to be introduced to Miss Hardcastle earlier than he had expected? Suddenly, his masterful manner crumbles into stammering, squirming timidity: 'What if we should postpone the happiness till tomorrow? – Tomorrow at her own house. – It will be every bit as convenient – and rather more respectful. – Tomorrow let it be' (260–61).

Before this first meeting, Marlow himself has given us an account of his strange personality, suggesting that his shyness with women of his own class is due to lack of confidence and unfamiliarity; with other women, though, he easily takes the role of would-be conqueror (251):

Marlow. My life has been chiefly spent in a college or an inn, in seclusion from that lovely part of the creation that chiefly teach men confidence. I don't know that I was ever familiarly acquainted with a single modest woman – except my mother – but among females of another class, you know –
Hastings. Ay, among them you are impudent enough of all conscience!

Just what is the source of Marlow's terror? He explains how in the presence of a pretty woman of his own class he becomes tongue-tied; in awe of feminine beauty he is lost for words: 'I'm doomed to adore the sex, and yet to converse with the only part of it I despise' (253). He calls his affliction the 'Englishman's malady' (251) and indeed it seems that in creating Marlow, Goldsmith is commenting upon the restrictions imposed on relationships between men and women in his time. Marlow simply lacks a suitable language, an appropriate manner, by which to express himself to a woman whom he might court. Women of a lower class present no such problem. Because they are not to be courted, they are simply objects of sexual conquest who offer Marlow a role he can easily play; he knows every line, every move. But with women of his own social station he has yet to learn the true language of love. How ironic it is that Marlow has more to gain than Kate from a system of arranged marriages!

It is through Kate that Marlow will find within himself the capacity to express his feelings to the object of his admiration – but only by accident. When they first meet, Marlow is consumed by embarrassed shyness, able only to blurt out unfinished platitudes, clichés he has picked up from the popular plays and novels of his time, hardly daring to look at the woman who is his intended bride. How different he is, though, when he glimpses her later in her housewife's dress and assumes she is the barmaid. Now he is on familiar ground: physically attracted to her, he is the smart young man-about-town determined on another conquest, full of rakish humour and self-confidence. His manner remains insolent with Mr Hardcastle – until the awful truth is forced upon him and he realizes his mistake. Ashamed and embarrassed, only Kate's quick thinking prevents him from leaving the house immediately; she pretends to be not the barmaid but 'A poor relation appointed to keep the keys, and to see that the guests want nothing in my power to give them' (288–9). Now we begin to see the best of Marlow: faced with a young woman to whom he has already (inadvertently) revealed his sexual attraction but who is not the coquettish plaything he took her for, he speaks and behaves with an unforced gracefulness and honour: '(*Aside.*) By heaven, she weeps. This is the first mark of tenderness I ever had from a modest woman, and it touches me. (*To her.*) Excuse me, my lovely girl, you are the only part of the family I leave with reluctance. But to be plain with you, the difference of our birth, fortune and education, make an honourable connexion impossible' (289–90). Realizing that she is a virtuous girl whom he could easily hurt further he resolves to quit the house.

Consequently he is understandably perplexed and angry when he finds his father and Mr Hardcastle teasing him about his 'success' with Kate Hardcastle. He defends himself stoutly and with the vigour of wounded pride: 'I saw the lady without emotion, and parted without reluctance. I hope you'll exact no further proofs of my duty, nor prevent me from leaving a house in which I suffer so many mortifications' (299). He has yet to be disabused of his final illusion; that comes with Kate's last deception when, still in the role of 'poor relation', she detains Marlow within the hearing of their two fathers. Now Marlow is finally able to reconcile the contradictions of his character: neither bashfully fearful nor swaggeringly impudent, he is able to express his love for her with true dignity and self-confidence (307). Anguish returns when Kate reveals her true identity, but by now Marlow has been led into winning a wife for himself and he can feel himself to be 'the happiest man alive' (311).

Marlow is a fortunate man. He possesses fine qualities of honesty, trustworthiness and affection which remain unfulfilled until Kate 'stoops to conquer' him. He is the dupe of both Tony and Kate: the London womanizer is humbled into happiness by a country bumpkin and a rustic girl. The tricks and misunderstandings surrounding Marlow are the source of much of the play's comedy; so are the extremes of his character. If we disapprove of his arrogance, we also pity his tormented shyness, so that our feelings about him are quite complex and shifting.

We approve of him in the end because we feel he has suffered enough to deserve his happiness.

GEORGE HASTINGS

George Hastings is a pleasant young man of easy temperament and sociability. In love with Constance Neville, he is to be introduced to her family by his friend Marlow but plans to elope with Constance and her modest fortune to France where they can be married (her now deceased father having already consented). Their plan would be threatened, though, if Marlow were to discover the 'inn' to be the house of his own intended bride, and so they have to keep him in ignorance for as long as possible.

We quickly learn that Hastings is much more at ease with people than Marlow, whose shyness still amazes him. He is taken aback at the extravagant politeness of Mr Hardcastle when he believes him to be the innkeeper but accepts it simply as an effort to please (258). He manages the first introduction between Marlow and Kate with easy gallantry and supports Marlow with encouraging words before withdrawing to conduct his own business. He uses his good manners all too easily to flatter Mrs Hardcastle with talk of London fashion and there is a sly humour in his teasing her so as to expose her real ignorance of such things.

We never doubt his true love for Constance: 'Perish the baubles! Your person is all I desire' (260) and when Marlow unwittingly returns the jewels to Mrs Hardcastle he remains outwardly composed. His anguish when his plot with Tony is discovered by Mrs Hardcastle is genuine: 'My heart! How can I support this? To be so near happiness, and such happiness!' (296), and he rounds in anger on Tony and Marlow. But he soon recovers his poise and, having agreed to Constance's arguments against elopement, behaves with manly dignity in his speech of apology to Mr Hardcastle (310).

Hastings has a natural sense of fairness, as when he accepts Tony Lumpkin's rebuke (302). As his name suggests, there is a streak of recklessness in his character, seen when he rounds on Tony with his sword half-drawn and in his eagerness to elope which Constance finally curbs. His main purpose in the play is, with his smooth manners and fashionable sophistication, to act as a contrast to Marlow and also to give us valuable information about his friend's character (e.g. 251–2). At the end of the play, he is commended by Sir Charles Marlow, and it is Hastings who finally enjoins Marlow and Kate: 'I know you like him, I'm sure he loves you, and you must and shall have him' (311).

SIR CHARLES MARLOW

An old friend of Mr Hardcastle, Sir Charles intends their two families to be united by the marriage of his son to Kate Hardcastle. His son appears to be rather in awe of him; it is to keep his father's approval that he at first considers marriage with Kate improper when he believes her to be a poor relation of the Hardcastles. On the other hand, this suggests a certain proper respectfulness and when Marlow declares his love for Kate he believes his father's good judgement will rightly appreciate her personal qualities (307).

We hear of Sir Charles's arrival in Act V; the first impression is that he is a good-hearted man, able to enjoy with Mr Hardcastle the embarrassment that has befallen his son. But he cannot believe the account Kate gives to him of his son's easy forwardness when she tells of his behaviour to her and is bitterly angry with Marlow when, secretly watching his passionate meeting with Kate, he thinks his son has deliberately deceived him (308). But his mood quickly changes when the full situation is revealed to him. He readily commends Hastings as a worthy fellow and enthusiastically praises Tony's renunciation of Constance: 'O brave 'squire!' (310).

Sir Charles, then, is an amiable character. He is not worried about the small size of Kate's fortune but is concerned only that there is a genuine affection between the young lovers (297). We have the impression of a mature man of wise understanding and sound judgement.

MINOR CHARACTERS

The minor characters include the servants and the 'low' characters at the Three Pigeons. Their main purpose is to help develop the plot, but they also provide a good deal of comedy.

The 'low' characters at the tavern are used to show how easily Tony, who is after all socially superior to them, is able to mix. They call Tony's boisterous song genteel and in attempting to be refined mock the genteel pretensions of the largely middle-class audience watching them. Tony is clearly comfortable with them and feels himself amongst equals.

As for the servants such as Roger and Diggory, whom Mr Hardcastle attempts to train, their comic ineptness is hilariously funny. The relationship between master and servants is informal and relaxed. They are farm-hands who are out of their depth trying to learn how to behave in genteel company but their simplicity is appealing. They serve to emphasize, along with other 'low' characters, the close bonds of affection that exist in Mr Hardcastle's rural retreat.

Commentary

COMEDY

When *She Stoops to Conquer* first appeared, the great Dr Johnson, Goldsmith's friend and admirer, gave the opinion that he knew of no comedy for many years 'that has so much exhilarated an audience, that has answered so much the great end of comedy – making an audience merry'. The play has continued to delight audiences ever since. It is peculiarly difficult to analyse comedy, to say just what it is about a character, a piece of dialogue, a situation which makes us laugh. We need to remember too, that the word 'comedy' means much more than the business of keeping us amused. Its larger meaning describes a situation in which characters who are beset by difficulties nevertheless win through to happiness. It is a movement towards the resolution of conflicts, the establishment of reconciliation and harmony, showing us that despite all its unforeseeable accidents and complexities, life can turn out for the best. The focus for this comic attitude is often the relationship between pairs of lovers who, having risen above misfortune, find their way towards the happiness traditionally enshrined by marriage. Comedy makes us laugh; it also makes us contented because it is essentially optimistic. Goldsmith's play is clearly a comedy in this larger sense: the two pairs of lovers, Hastings and Constance, Marlow and Kate, survive misfortune and near-disaster to achieve the happiness promised by marriage.

One of the things that makes us laugh is the way people behave in the play. Consider, for example, Mrs Hardcastle. She tries to hide her monstrous selfishness behind the façade of sophistication and civilized good taste. The flimsiness of that façade, the ease and regularity with which it crumbles, make us laugh. We catch a glimpse of this in the play's first scene when, after trying to excuse Tony's behaviour to her husband, she ends up physically battling with her beloved son. Her pretensions to fashion and cosmopolitan manners are most effectively exposed by Hastings; she knows nothing of London except what she has managed to pick up from the magazines. In fact, all her attempts to appear fashionable spring from her personal vanity: 'I'm in love with the town, and that serves to raise me above some of our neighbouring rustics' (265). But the mask of elegance and good breeding is perpetually slipping and we laugh at the regularity with which, try as she might to hide it, her real nature shows itself. For example, early in Act III she tries calmly and with all the appearance of kindness to persuade Constance that jewels are unfashionable and that their having gone missing is of no importance. But moments later, when she has discovered that the jewels are indeed gone, her vindictive fury confirms for us that the jewels are, as we always supposed, of great importance to her.

Another source of the play's comedy is the behaviour of the 'low' characters: Tony's chums at the Three Pigeons and Mr Hardcastle's servants. Good comic actors would make a great deal of the opportunities for knockabout fun and comic business in the inn scene. Similarly, the scene in which Mr Hardcastle tries to prepare his servants for Marlow's arrival has ample scope for comic acting. Here is the somewhat fussy and nervous Mr Hardcastle trying, with military briskness, to teach his dull-witted farm-hands in the space of a few minutes how to behave at table in genteel company. He himself collapses into gales of laughter when reminded of a favourite funny story by his servant. His attempts at training come to nothing when, at the crucial moment, the servants scatter as Marlow arrives.

Apart from characters' behaviour, the play's dialogue often provokes our laughter. Here it is Tony who is often to the fore. His mental agility is accompanied by a verbal inventiveness. When he gives Marlow instructions to reach Mr Hardcastle's house, he takes delight in long-windedly pointing out the obvious (245) and in inventing an impossibly complicated route full of frightening names like 'Crack-skull common'. Towards the end of the play, he teases Hastings by not telling him directly where he has left Mrs Hardcastle and Constance but instead leading him to the truth by clever riddles (301). The same liveliness of language is to be seen when Tony gives his description of Constance to

Hastings not knowing, of course, that he is talking to a man deeply in love with her: 'there's not a more bitter cantankerous toad in all Christendom!' (268). A similar comic misunderstanding arises when Mr Hardcastle, anxious to join in the two young men's conversation, mistakes their talk of 'opening campaigns', 'wanting ammunition' and 'securing a retreat' for a military conversation close to his own heart (254). He does not know that the campaign under discussion is a sexual one and that one of its targets is his own daughter!

FARCE

Much of our laughter arises from the way in which ridiculous situations are piled one on top of another. The play's hectic action springs from a simple mistake, that of Marlow's conviction that the house of his intended father-in-law is actually an inn. From this follows a train of situations in which the characters, whether or not they think they know the truth, are in fact completely at sea. Mr Hardcastle cannot understand why the reputedly modest Marlow is so casual and impudent; Marlow cannot understand why the 'innkeeper' is so attentive and intrusive; he tries to seduce a barmaid, finds he has fallen in love with a poor relation of the Hardcastles and then discovers that the simple girl for whom he falls to his knees is the genteel young woman to whom he earlier could not utter a sentence. The same sort of improbabilities and coincidences are to be found in the Mrs Hardcastle–Hastings–Constance plot. The jewels that Mrs Hardcastle pretends are mislaid have indeed been stolen and the trick she arranged with Tony now traps her; Constance inadvertently tricks Tony into believing her invented contents of Hastings's letter, thereby allowing Mrs Hardcastle to discover the planned elopement; Tony's tormenting of his bedraggled mother with pretended glimpses of highwaymen becomes real torment when his stepfather arrives on the scene, and he in turn finds his distraught wife falling at his feet to beg for the life of her son.

Now, all these situations are funny because we know more of the truth than the characters do. We see them caught up in situations beyond their control and laugh at their helplessness. The action relies

on a degree of improbability, coincidence, capricious accident. It is
tempting, then, to think of the play as a farce. A farce is a dramatic
work which aims only at exciting laughter by exploiting ridiculous and
absurd dramatic situations without much regard to plausibility. Farce
depends for its effects on extravagant comic invention, knockabout
buffoonery and rapid action: it has little to do with convincing characterization or with the development of ideas and emotions. It is true that
some of the incidents in Goldsmith's play are unlikely or far-fetched,
but given the nature of the characters he has invented they are never
entirely implausible or impossible. And while there are moments of
near farce, the play contains much more than a succession of comic
situations. There is skill and art of the highest order in the creation of
characters we can believe in, in the economy and wit of the dialogue,
in the development of our sympathies for certain characters. The play
is immeasurably richer and more substantial than a farce could ever be.
Its rapid action and comic timing owe something to farce, but the play
is a brilliant comedy, not a farce.

DISGUISE AND ILLUSION

The mainspring of the comic action is trickery: either characters trick
one another by disguising themselves in some way, or else they deceive
themselves by believing something to be what it is not. Examples are
numerous. Marlow is tricked into believing the house is an inn; he is
tricked by Kate about her identity as a barmaid and then as a poor
relation. Tony helps Hastings and Constance disguise their love by
pretending affection for Constance to trick Mrs Hardcastle, who herself
tries to trick Constance out of her jewels, only to find she in turn has
been tricked by Tony who had already stolen them. Tony and Constance
are then trapped by Constance's trick with the letter; he redeems the
situation by tricking his mother into believing they are travelling away
from the house when in fact he is travelling around it. Mr Hardcastle
is perpetually deceived. Firstly, he is forced by Marlow's behaviour to
the conclusion that Marlow is an impudent young pup; when this
mistake is cleared away he falls into another illusion. Having seen

Marlow passionately embrace Kate, he then listens in astonishment while Marlow explains to him and to Sir Charles that his relations with Kate are cool and reserved, and then secretly watches Marlow unreservedly expressing his passion to his daughter. Both Mr Hardcastle and Sir Charles are led to the seemingly inescapable conclusion that Marlow has set out to deceive them. They are wrong, of course; it is Mr Hardcastle's faithful, dutiful daughter who has tricked them all. We might remember, too, that it is Mr Hardcastle's peculiar insistence on Kate wearing a plain dress that furthers Marlow's illusion that the house is an inn, which then sets in train the process by which Marlow falls in love with Kate and so leads us to the play's happy resolution.

Only one character in the play fails to be tricked, and that is Kate. She practises deception but is never fooled herself. All the other deceivers are at some point themselves deceived: Constance, Hastings, Mrs Hardcastle, Tony all fall prey either to someone else's or their own trickery. Mr Hardcastle and Marlow are the perpetual dupes, stumbling unwittingly from one illusion to another. Kate remains untouched and unharmed, the only character in control of the Mistakes of a Night. Her shrewdness, common sense, intelligence, wit and resourcefulness, and ultimately her natural kindness and warmth, keep her safe from the surrounding deception.

APPEARANCE AND REALITY

The play presents us, then, with a succession of complex intrigues and stratagems by which characters deceive one another or are themselves deceived. In this play nothing is ever as it seems and the characters are caught up in a web of subterfuge. Always subject to other people's ploys and designs, all the characters except Kate experience various degrees of bewilderment. Appearances are deceptive, and the truth, the reality, is hard to perceive. All comes right in the end (except for Mrs Hardcastle) but only by virtue of Kate's wisdom. Tony, too, plays his part in bringing about the final happiness. Both he and Kate are inventive in their tricks, but where Tony's wit is mocking, even destructive, hers is restorative and kindly. Her wisdom lies in her acceptance that the truth is not always visible, that surfaces do not reveal all, that appearances can obscure reality. Her reaction after that disastrous first interview with Marlow is not contempt or mockery, but laughter. She has seen behind his bashfulness, has probed beneath the surface manner of timid modesty and perceived that 'He has good sense, but then so buried in his fears, that it fatigues one more than ignorance' (264). Marlow's manner, she correctly judges, is born out of his fear of women, and she sets about helping him overcome that fear. Later, when persuading her father that he may have been misled in his view of Marlow, she states 'And yet there may be many good qualities under that first appearance' (272). Only Kate could say this, and the play fully bears her out as characters, gradually, and sometimes painfully, learn that the truth is not always what it appears to be.

This theme of appearance and reality runs deep in the play. Every character either deliberately or accidentally gives a false impression of themselves or receives a false impression of another character. Everybody appears to be something they are not. Marlow and Hastings take Tony for a tedious country bumpkin when they enter the Three Pigeons, and they treat him accordingly, unable to recognize that Tony Lumpkin is in fact the squire and thus of their own class. Mr Hardcastle, with his old-fashioned hospitality, is easily mistaken for an innkeeper who tries to be a gentleman; in reality, he is a gentleman, of 'one of the best families in the country' (289). Mrs Hardcastle tries to give the impression of well-bred sophistication; in reality she is a vain, selfish simpleton. Only too late does she discover that Constance is not an innocent, dutiful niece to be manipulated at will and that Hastings, the elegant, smooth-talking young Londoner is actually plotting elopement and thinks of her as 'the hag' (293). At the same time, it is Mrs Hardcastle who also surprises us in showing a selfless courage when she thinks Tony is being attacked by a highwayman. Kate is far from the submissive, passively dutiful daughter her father thinks her; she can also be the coquettish barmaid who so excites and misleads Marlow. And as only she knows, Marlow is not entirely what he appears to be. He is more than the shyly stammering young man she first sees; he is more than the impudent, swaggering bully that Mr Hardcastle takes him for; he is more than the bold seducer of barmaids. Marlow is, in fact, all appearance. He behaves according to how he thinks he *ought* to behave, projecting an image of himself he thinks appropriate to the situation. He relies on his social superiority, on his power to command and on his money. With the supposed innkeeper he is high-handed: 'It's my house. This is my house. Mine, while I choose to stay. What right have you to bid me leave this house, sir?' (287). With the supposed barmaid he is predatory and even violent. Only through Kate does he discover his true character when he drops to his knees in submission, finally able to express genuine feeling. The play shows that we are not what we seem to other people; sometimes, we are not what we seem to ourselves.

SATIRE

Many of the play's characters, then, have something to learn about themselves. Goldsmith is, in fact, satirizing certain features of human behaviour. Satire is the name given to the sort of comedy that sets out to expose the foibles and failings of human behaviour by ridiculing it. In order to make such behaviour appear ridiculous, it is exaggerated and we laugh at it. Such comedy makes us laugh, but it also teaches us something about ourselves; in its aim to improve us, satire is moral as well as funny.

An obvious object of such satire is Marlow: the extremes of his behaviour, his modesty and his boldness, are exaggerated so that we laugh at them. But we also learn that such behaviour is foolish and even damaging. Marlow has to be led into finding a middle way between these extremes. But he is not the only character whose faults are exposed. Mr Hardcastle is, for the most part, a sympathetic and likeable character. We quickly see his resigned affection for his foolish wife and the mutual trust and respect between him and Kate. He is kind to his servants and probably has more in common with them than with his genteel young guests. But there is a grain of complacency and self-satisfaction in his character. He could easily be an old bore and is a little too prone to sententious moralizing, as when he reprimands Kate for her finery: 'I could never teach the fools of this age, that the indigent world could be clothed out of the trimmings of the vain' (239). He rather too easily accepts things at face value. For example, so long as Kate fulfils her part of their bargain and wears her housewife's dress in the evening, her father never suspects she is anything other than his dutiful daughter whose obedience he is to test by the introduction of Marlow as a suitor (239). But it is significant that Goldsmith uses Kate's plain clothes as a device to keep Mr Hardcastle in tormented confusion right to the end of the play (since Marlow mistakes her for a barmaid). By making Kate's *dress* the cause of further confusion, Goldsmith is reminding us that appearances can be deceptive: Kate's clothes deceive Marlow, just as her outward manner of passive obedience (seen, for example, at the end of Act III) can mislead her father. We might note, too, that Mr Hardcastle's first words to Kate, 'my pretty innocence' (239), are precisely echoed by Mrs Hardcastle at the moment when she is being tricked by Tony and Constance (291). Kate is far from disobedient, but neither is she quite as innocent as Mr Hardcastle believes. She marries the man chosen for her by her father not simply out of a sense of duty but only when after many complications she herself has discovered Marlow to be worthy of her.

Goldsmith also makes great fun of what Mr Hardcastle first says about Marlow. Describing him to Kate, Mr Hardcastle celebrates the fact that Marlow is 'one of the most bashful and reserved young fellows in all the world'. In answer to Kate's natural disappointment, he trots out a comfortable platitude: 'modesty seldom resides in a breast that is not enriched with nobler virtues' (240). This sentimental notion is turned against him with a vengeance! The modest Marlow will, one way or another, torment Mr Hardcastle for the rest of the play. And yet it is also true that alongside Marlow's modesty there are indeed nobler virtues of honour and affection. Mr Hardcastle is not wrong, it is simply that his sweeping statement cannot express the whole truth; life is more complex than his platitudes can express.

Constance and Hastings also have something to learn about themselves. Hastings is in the mould of the romantic lover, impetuous and careless of practical necessity. His cry of 'Perish the baubles! Your person is all I desire' (260) is good for romantic heroes of fiction, but not for young lovers who have to live in the real world, as Constance knows, for she is unwilling to leave without her jewels. Moreover, at the moment of liberation, when Hastings is urging elopement, Constance refuses it. This is partly due to her exhaustion after Tony's drive, but also to a hard-headed realism which is the opposite of Hastings's enthusiastic romanticism: 'Prudence once more comes to my relief, and I will obey its dictates. In the moment of passion, fortune may be despised, but it ever produces a lasting repentance' (305).

Tony, too, may have learned something from the mistakes of the night. We feel great warmth for his energy and vivacity but there is a moment in the play, at the end of Act IV, when it appears that his tricks and mischief have led to disaster. It is he who recovers the situation and at the play's end he gains his reward in the form of his inheritance, but he does not entirely escape Goldsmith's satire. Tony lives for the moment, for the instant gratification of whims and desires. We see this on his first entrance when he refuses to let his mother detain him from the pleasures of meeting his friends at the Three Pigeons: 'As for disappointing them I should not so much mind; but I can't abide to disappoint myself!' (239). He does not think about the consequences of his actions and so is perpetually extricating himself from tight corners. We do not criticize him for this: he is incorrigible and irrepressible and will always survive on his wits. But, rather like Hastings, his impulsiveness can lead him into danger. Hastings needs guidance; Tony will always be able to save himself but we may feel that, now he has been granted adult status, Tony at the end of the play will be rather more responsible and less childish than Tony at the beginning. He will never change, but his energies might find a less disruptive outlet.

Mrs Hardcastle's vanities and affectations are an obvious target of Goldsmith's satire. Her selfishness is boundless, her foolishness glaringly obvious to everyone but herself. Ultimately, she is too self-centred and insensitive to learn anything or to change. Oblivious to everything except herself and her own interests, Mrs Hardcastle is used by Goldsmith to show how gross and ridiculous self-regard can become. And if Mrs Hardcastle can learn nothing, then we feel that Kate has nothing to learn. She is the one major character who is beyond Goldsmith's satirical gaze.

YOUTH AND AGE

At the heart of drama is conflict, conflict between people or within an individual. Broadly speaking, a drama whose conflict ends in waste and destruction is tragedy; conflict which is resolved leads to comedy.

The conflicts in *She Stoops to Conquer* fall into a clear pattern: it is the conflict between youth and age, between a younger generation and its parents. All the youthful characters, Kate, Marlow, Tony, Constance and Hastings, are in some way trapped. Kate is trapped by her father's old-fashioned obsessions and his expectation that she will fall in with his choice of suitor (she has to resign herself to making the best of Marlow on first learning of his extreme bashfulness) even though he will not absolutely control her decision. Tony is trapped by his mother; denied his fortune and independence, he is locked into prolonged childhood. Constance and Hastings are trapped by Mrs Hardcastle's avarice, which will not permit Constance's fortune to go outside the family. Marlow is trapped by his father's desire that he will marry the daughter of an old family friend even though Marlow himself is terrified at the prospect of courtship, trapped by an over-concern with other people's opinion of him and trapped, too, by the conventions of courtship and a view of women which render him paralysed with fear before an intended bride. Marlow is liberated from his incapacities by Kate, who, like others of her generation, is forced to resort to subterfuge and deception as a means of liberation.

Mr Hardcastle is the most extreme example of how the older generation, however kindly and well-intentioned, obstructs the younger. Goldsmith stresses Mr Hardcastle's attachment to the past: his clothes, his wig, his conversation all belong to a bygone era. By contrast, his wife makes ridiculous efforts to belong to the present. Her attempts to be fashionable, to be *à la mode*, make her absurd. Both husband and wife are obsessive, one about the past, the other about the present.

To the younger generation belongs all the spirit and vivacity of youth: its optimism, confidence and robustness. Kate and Marlow, Hastings, Constance and Tony eventually achieve liberation from their parents and guardians, embarking on a future that now truly belongs to them. But the victory is not one-sided; it is not the case that the conflict is resolved because of a capitulation. The older generation may, in varying degrees, look foolish. Mrs Hardcastle is plainly foolish, Mr Hardcastle partly so, but Sir Charles Marlow certainly is not. He is, at the play's conclusion, momentarily mistaken about his son's behaviour, but he is fully sensible of Kate's virtues, declaring her the one he 'most wished for a daughter'. Kate, too, recognizes that here is a man she must respect, and there is no dissimulation in her reply: 'I am proud of your approbation . . .' (306). The young succeed, but not by simple rebellion. Goldsmith was a firm conservative in his thinking, and he was very far from the opinion that it is the duty of the present to overthrow the past. He valued continuity: Tony Lumpkin, after all, is welcomed by the 'low' characters at the inn because he resembles his father, the old squire, so closely. Moreover, Constance and Hastings do not elope, but return in order to do the proper thing, to seek the approval of Mr Hardcastle. It is quickly and easily granted, and we feel that this is right and just. In the final moments of the play, the young are granted their inheritance, the future. The two men are united with their partners and Tony receives his fortune. But it is Mr Hardcastle, that representative of a dying generation, who grants them their wishes. Of Constance and Hastings, he declares that he is 'glad they're come back to reclaim their due' (310); he tells Tony the truth about his age and it is he who joins the hands of Kate and Marlow. The conflict ends not in overthrow or supremacy, but in the integration and harmony of the past with the future.

LOVE

Love is one of the driving forces of the play. Hastings plans to elope with Constance; Marlow accidentally falls in love with Kate; Tony wins his freedom to pursue Bet Bouncer. Obstacles which have to be overcome are placed in the paths of these lovers. Constance cannot get her hands on her own fortune, Tony is encumbered by his mother's determination that he should marry his cousin and Marlow's bashful modesty makes him incapable of wooing a suitable wife. Being a comedy, the play finally brings the lovers together after they have surmounted their difficulties. As it is presented in the play, love is not a terribly profound or mysterious emotion, but the play does show us different varieties of love and the dangers attending each of them.

The most complex case is Marlow's. He knows only two attitudes to women: either they are untouchable goddesses whose very presence paralyses him with fear or they are playthings in the game of seduction. The play shows us his divided character. With Kate Hardcastle he is tongue-tied; with the 'barmaid' he is swaggeringly confident. He only discovers a 'middle way', with a reconciliation of these opposed attitudes, when Kate pretends to be the poor relation. As such, she is not so socially elevated to be frightening to Marlow, nor is she so lowly as to be simply the object of his lust. Besides, by the time she pretends to Marlow that she is the poor relation, he has already, though inadvertently, revealed to her a frankly sexual desire. This for Marlow is the crucial breakthrough. He treats women of his own class with cold remoteness, as if terrified of revealing to them any sign of sexual attraction. To him, such women are not flesh and blood, but awe-inspiring statues. We can see this attitude in his first meeting with Kate (261–4).

In her presence, he automatically adopts a manner of profound gravity and moral seriousness. After Hastings has abandoned his friend, Kate teases Marlow by suggesting that he must be used to conversing with ladies. Marlow's reply is suitably self-effacing: 'Pardon me, madam, I- I- I- as yet have studied–only–to–deserve them' (262). To this suggestion, Kate's reply is realistic and shrewd: 'And that some say is the very worst way to obtain them' (262). A man who feels that only by revering a woman is she likely to notice him is probably going to find himself ignored rather than admired. As the stuttering conversation develops, Marlow tries to achieve the elevated moral tone of a 'man of sentiment', that hero of contemporary popular fiction who, overwhelmed by the world's cruelty and hypocrisy, spent his life practising acts of pious virtue and secretly feeling very pleased with himself. Such a man, possessed of profound humility, would not feel himself worthy to approach a refined woman (although in fiction they conveniently fall at his feet). Again, Kate shrewdly makes a telling point: '... a want of courage upon some occasions assumes the appearance of ignorance, and betrays us when we most want to excel' (263–4). In the real world of men and women, an attitude of indifference to the natural appetites and healthy desires of flesh and blood is likely to leave you out in the cold. And this is the danger facing Marlow. Until he recognizes that refined women such as Kate are not a race apart, until he can make himself vulnerable by revealing his feelings to them, he is likely to remain a spectator of rather than a participant in life.

With women of a different class, these dangers do not arise. But there are dangers of a different sort. When Hastings reminds Marlow of his 'impudence' with such certain women, Marlow replies 'They are of *us*, you know' (252). He regards them as fellow-participants in a game whose rules are well known. Such women are to be played with and cast aside, and in Marlow's view they are as willing and as casual in their attitude as their rakish seducers. Such an attitude not only denies any access of real feeling and human emotion, it also suggests that Marlow hardly regards such women as women at all, but rather as fellow-creatures in the game of sex. With such an attitude, Marlow will never achieve a deep and satisfying relationship.

But when he encounters Kate in her guise of poor relation, he finds a woman to whom he has easily expressed physical attraction and who has responded to him with equal warmth. He sees Kate neither as a remote statue, nor as a plaything, and the way is clear for him to discover the deep emotions which lie within him. True, he does not know that he is addressing Kate Hardcastle, but that hardly matters; he is addressing, with manly passion, a woman for whom he feels deeply and to whom he has already expressed a sexual attraction.

Hastings's case is different. He has no such problems in dealing with women easily and naturally. The dangers facing him are the dangers of romantic hot-headedness. His feelings for Constance are passionate. Marlow is to furnish him an introduction to the family: 'Miss Neville loves you, the family don't know you; as my friend you are sure of a reception, and let honour do the rest' (253). It is not clear whether Marlow knows of the plan to elope; certainly, Hastings's grateful reply gives no hint of it. Only when he meets Constance does he announce his intentions: 'if my dearest girl will trust in her faithful Hastings, we shall soon be landed in France, where even among slaves the laws of marriage are respected' (259). Constance, however, is not so eager and wants to delay long enough to acquire her jewels from Mrs Hardcastle.

It is not quite clear why Hastings is in such a tearing hurry. He tells us that her now deceased father had consented to the marriage, Constance herself is plainly willing to marry him and her fortune is of no consequence to him: 'Perish the baubles! Your person is all I desire' (260). The single impediment is that Constance is not yet of age and so would require permission to marry from her guardian, Mrs Hardcastle; on that score, we know that Mrs Hardcastle would refuse, given her determination to marry her niece to her son, Tony. But it is made clear very early in the play that both Tony and Constance will resist Mrs Hardcastle's persuasions. 'But at any rate, if my dear Hastings be but constant, I make no doubt to be too hard for her at last' (242). What we have to ask, then, is whether Hastings's urgency suggests that he is incapable of constancy. We do not doubt his passion for Constance; what we must doubt is its endurance. The test comes towards the end of the play, when Constance is led off to virtual imprisonment with her Aunt Pedigree. Her parting words are a reminder to Hastings that he must remain constant for three years until she comes of age (296). Given what we know of Hastings's impulsive nature, that might well prove very difficult for him. In the end, the matter is resolved when Constance is restored to him. Now more clear-sighted, she realizes that undue haste in love may lose much more than it gains: 'Two or three years' patience will at last crown us with happiness' (305). Hastings resists: 'Such a tedious delay is worse than inconstancy. Let us fly, my charmer' (305). But Constance is the stronger; she will not be moved and resolves to trust to Mr Hardcastle's influence for success. With Tony's renunciation of her and her aunt's plans destroyed, Constance's better judgement earns its reward.

When it comes to young love, the women of the play are far wiser than the men. Kate and Constance lead their partners to a better understanding of what love is by showing them what it is not. It is not a timid reverence; nor is it a game of sexual combat; nor is it the short-lived heat of impulsiveness. We might recall Tony's description of Bet Bouncer: 'two eyes as black as sloes, and cheeks as broad and red as a pulpit cushion' (269). There we see something of the natural, vigorous and robust quality that truly belongs to love.

TOWN AND COUNTRY

The play begins with the opposition between town and country, with Mrs Hardcastle longing to visit the sophistication of London and Mr Hardcastle's attack on its vanities and follies. The play itself takes place entirely within the confines of Mr Hardcastle's house and the surrounding countryside but, with the introduction of Marlow and Hastings, we have the presence of the values of the town to set against the values of the country.

Tony Lumpkin best embodies the qualities of the country. He is energetically healthy and fond of outdoor pursuits, and prefers the robust Bet Bouncer to the more elegant Constance. His vocabulary is shot through with rustic dialect and images drawn from the countryside. Into the Three Pigeons come Marlow and Hastings from the sophisticated and elegant society of London. Immediately, their clothes, manner and way of speaking mark them out as different from Tony, even though they are of the same social status. Their somewhat offhand, patronizing attitude annoys Tony, and when they refer to him by reputation as 'an awkward booby' he decides to give them their come-uppance. His description of the supposed route to Mr Hardcastle's house is designed to disconcert the two Londoners with the terrors lurking in unknown countryside. References to rutted tracks that can overthrow horses and navigation by local landmarks are reminders to the two sophisticates that despite their swaggering manners they are in an environment which is not their own.

Another point of contrast between town and country comes at the end of Act IV. Hastings, Marlow and Constance round on Tony as the cause of their misfortune. Throwing insults at Tony, Marlow and Hastings strike the appropriate attitude by drawing their swords, before turning to heap blame on each other. As Constance's distress increases, the two friends continue to quarrel until she pleads with them to be pacified. It seems that the fashionable young men are, for a moment, more intent on standing on their honour than in attending to Constance's distress or facing the reality of the situation. Later, when Tony has rescued Constance, he reminds the suitably grateful Hastings of how, not too long ago, 'it was all idiot, cub, and run me through the guts'. Had Hastings been in earnest earlier, Tony would now be dead and

Hastings facing the gallows. 'Damn your way of fighting, I say. After we take a knock in this part of the country, we kiss and be friends' (302). The rebuke, as Hastings acknowledges, is just. Through Tony, Goldsmith is suggesting not that men like Hastings are ready to run people through, but that their notion of honour is self-centred and just a little vain. Inciting duels may be swashbuckling and seemingly heroic, but a sword and a hot temper can bring about tragic consequences and it is Tony's view of the matter which offers the saner, more humane approach.

With the betrothal of Marlow and Kate, and Hastings and Constance, comes the reconciliation of town and country. Since the two major agents of the plot, Tony and Kate, are also country-bred characters, it is not difficult to perceive that Goldsmith's sympathies are with the older, gentler values of the country rather than the gaudy, restless appeal of the town. The character of Mrs Hardcastle makes this clear; in love with the town, she is the most unlovely character in the play. We end with the promise of celebration: 'Tomorrow we shall gather all the poor of the parish about us' (311) and we feel that a country wedding in this age-old, tightly-knit corner of rural England is the only fitting conclusion.

Glossary

above-stairs: upstairs (i.e. in her bedroom)
all upon the high rope!: i.e. 'on his high horse!'
allons: (Fr.) let's go
Ally Cawn: Nawab of Bengal; he had been defeated in a battle in 1764
Ally Croaker: character in a popular Irish ballad
Aminabad: in the Bible, the father-in-law of Aaron; also eighteenth-century
  slang for a Quaker
anon?: pardon?
answer for: take responsibility for
argue down a single button: Mr Hardcastle continues to wear unfashionably
  long waistcoats
Ariadne: opera by Handel (1685–1759)
at the top: i.e. at the head of the table

bagatelle: a trifle
bandbox: box for holding ribbons, trinkets, etc.; hence showy, cosmetic
bar cant: slang used by bar *habitués*
basket: the outside back seat of a carriage, used also to carry luggage
baskets: sticks resembling swords with protective wicker handguards
Battle of Belgrade: the siege of Belgrade in 1717 by which Prince Eugene
  defeated a Turkish army
baubles: worthless trinkets
bauld: dialect for 'bold'
Bayes: a reference to Mr Bayes, the hero of Buckingham's play *The Rehearsal*
  (1672); also a pun on 'bays' – wreaths of bay laurel were used as a mark of
  distinction for victorious athletes in ancient Greece and, later, metaphorically
  for poets (hence Poet Laureate)
bear your charges: pay your expenses
Bedlam: the lunatic asylum in St George's Fields, London
before faces: in front of other people
behind the scenes: off-stage
bekeays: dialect for 'because'
billing: kissing
blade: gallant, dashing fellow (indicated by the wearing of a sword)
blocks: featureless wooden heads used as stands to keep wigs in shape

bobs: ear-rings

booby: foolish lout

Borough: the borough of Southwark, inhabited by well-to-do tradesmen and the site of a disreputable market

bounce of a cracker: bang of a firework

breaking: breaking in, training (a horse)

Bully Dawson: an infamous London ruffian of the day

burning mountain: Vesuvius erupted in 1767

buzz: confusion

by the elevens: an exclamation perhaps referring to the twelve Apostles with the exception of Judas

canting: loose, informal

caricatura: cartoon-style drawings of famous people were displayed in print shops

caro: (It.) dear; hence 'excellent', 'Bravo!'

cat and fiddle!: nonsense!

catherine wheel: rotating firework, so called after St Catherine of Alexandria, martyred on a spiked wheel (AD 307)

cattle: horses

Che faro: song from Gluck's opera *Orpheus and Eurydice*

Cherry in Beaux' Stratagem: Cherry was the landlord's daughter in George Farquhar's popular play *The Beaux' Stratagem* (1707)

chit: young woman

chop-house: popular eating place

Cicero: the Roman statesman and orator (143–106 BC)

circumbendibus: roundabout way

cits: citizens

college bed-maker: domestic servant in residential college

come to his own: succeded in his inheritance

comet: one had appeared in 1769

comic muse: Thalia, one of the nine muses in Greek mythology

complete housewife: a popular magazine giving domestic tips

concatenation: a chain of connected things or ideas (the use here is nonsensical)

connexion: personal relationship

consumptive: ill; more particularly, afflicted by tuberculosis

coquets: flirts with, teases

coursing me through Quincy: following a course of treatment in Dr John Quincy's *Compleat English Dispensatory*, a well-known book of home remedies

court of King Solomon at a puppet-show: King Solomon's court was renowned for its lavish wealth and opulence, which in a puppet show would be exaggerated by cheap and gaudy imitation

courted by proxy: courtship conducted by a go-between leading to an arranged marriage

coxcomb: impudent, conceited person
crack: lie
cross-grained: bad-tempered, obstinate
crown: five-shilling piece
cup: i.e. drink

Darby . . . and Joan: any ageing, affectionate couple; from a ballad, 'The Happy Old Couple'
dashed: shame-faced, embarrassed
dégagée: (Fr.) nonchalant
Denain: town in Flanders where the allies were defeated by the French in 1713. Marlborough was certainly not there; neither, it seems, was Mr Hardcastle, whose story is nonsense
done my business: brought things to a conclusion
down: i.e. down from London
drab: slut, prostitute
draggled: doses
duchesses of Drury-Lane: prostitutes plying their trade in the area of the Theatre Royal, Drury Lane
Duke of Marlborough: John Churchill (1650–1722), first Duke of Marlborough, the greatest English general of his age
dullissimo: a coined word – the Italian ending *-issimo* means 'most', 'very'

Ecod: corruption of 'Egad', a mild oath
exciseman: collector of taxes on imported goods

father-in-law: stepfather
feeder: man who fattened cattle for slaughter; here, a trainer of fighting cocks
find out the longitude: since 1713 a prize of £20,000 had been offered by Parliament for the discovery of the mathematical means by which to determine longitude. (The prize was won in 1773, shortly after this play opened)
flaxen wig: long, heavy wigs were old-fashioned; small wigs were more popular, and some men wore none at all
Florentine: a baked dish of meat or fruit
fopperies: affectations, pretensions
'for us that sell ale': the reference is obscure: possibly it is to a popular song or to the buying and selling of votes in elections. Either way, it confirms the illusion that Mr Hardcastle is an innkeeper
fortin: fortune
frippery: cheap finery
friseur: (Fr.) hairdresser
furniture: accomplishments (with suggestion of sexual prowess)

garnets: semi-precious stones resembling rubies

gauze: thin, transparent material

genius: knowledge

good house-keeping: lavish hospitality

Gothic: uncivilized, barbarous

green and yellow dinner: probably a reference to elaborate sauces or highly coloured plates that try to compensate for inadequate food

Grotto Gardens: in Southwark, notorious as a place of amusement and far from fashionable

Grouse: common name for a dog

grumbletonian: grumbler

haspicholls: harpsichord

head: hairstyle in which the hair was mounted into a peak over a frame (and so was highly elaborate)

Heinel: Anna-Frederica Heinel was famous for the dances that she performed during operatic interludes

Heyder Ally: Sultan of Mysore, south India (1761–82); the British government was facing uprisings in India at this time

holds out: resists

humour: high spirits (also carrying an older sense of personal disposition)

I never nicked seven ... three times following: a reference to gambling on dice; having bet on a seven (using two dice), he would throw three times, scoring only two ones each time

improvements: alterations to landscaped gardens

in face: looking attractive

incontinently: immediately

India Director: a Director of the East India Company, which governed much of India and made vast fortunes

inflame a reckoning: increase a bill

inoculation: to prevent smallpox, contagious pus from an afflicted person was introduced into a healthy one to build up immunity. Vaccination came in 1779

intrepidity: audacity, daring

izzard: the letter z

Joiners' Company ... Corporation of Bedford: trade guilds and city councils were noted for their sumptuous feasts

jorum: punch bowl

kiss the hangman: go to the gallows (condemned criminals kissed the hangman as a sign of forgiveness)

knock himself down: bang his mallet (to call for silence)

knocked out: omitted

ladies' club: a fashionable club that met in Albemarle Street, London, in the 1770s; it admitted selected male guests

Ladies' Memorandum-book: magazine of ladies' fashions, first published in 1773

Lady Mayoress: the wife the Lord Mayor (the term did not then signify a lady mayor)

laurels: emblem of victory, after the ancient Greek custom of crowning victors with laurels

laws of marriage: the Royal Marriage Act of 1772 was passed to prevent the relations of the king from marrying at will; regarded as an infringement of personal liberties, it was highly unpopular

Lethes ... Styxes ... Stygians: in Greek mythology Lethe was the river of forgetfulness in Hades, the Underworld; Styx was the river over which the spirits of the dead were ferried. (Stygian is the adjective from Styx)

levy contributions: forced to finance itself

liberty and Fleet-Street: Fleet Street was the site of numerous inns

Liberty Hall: i.e. a place where you may do as you please. The phrase is taken from a famous Latin comedy by Plautus (250–184 BC)

Lion ... Angel ... Lamb: names given to rooms at an inn

lock-a-daisy: corruption of 'Alack the day!', a common expression of dismay

low: vulgar

maccaroni: name given to young men who dressed extravagantly and affected a passion for macaroni; hence, a dandy

made dishes: food made up of several ingredients

make a shift: have a go

make money of that: reckon it up

man of sentiment: man of deep feeling and sympathy

manner: refinement

marcasites: polished crystals resembling gold or silver

masquerade: masked ball

mauvaise honte: (Fr.) bashful manner

Methodist preachers: itinerant preachers who followed the teachings of Charles and John Wesley, urging clean living (including teetotalism) and noted for their emotional style of preaching

militia: citizens' army

Mistakes of a Night, The: the subtitle of Shakespeare's *A Midsummer Night's Dream*, a comedy also concerned with love and mistaken identity

modest: virtuous, respectable

Morrice! prance!: get out quickly (referring to the cry of the hobby-horse in Morris dances)

Mrs: the terms 'Mrs' and 'Miss' (contraction of 'mistress') were interchangeable, although 'Mrs', when applied to a young woman, often expressed disapproval

Mrs Mantrap, Lady Betty Blackleg ... Miss Biddy Buckskin: a formidable collection of women: a man-trap is a gin trap designed to catch poachers; a black-leg is a card-sharper; Biddy Buckskin refers to Rachel Lloyd, a prominent member of the ladies' club

mun: dialect for 'must'

muster: military inspection

Nancy Dawson: popular dancer well-known for her hornpipe

nectar: in Greek mythology, the drink of the gods

obstropalous: obstreperous, objectionable

of a size: of the same height

Oh lud!: Oh Lord!

omnes: (Lat.) all

Pantheon: a superior tea-house in Oxford Street

particular: peculiar

paste: artificial gem

pawn: stake

pigeon: slang word for a dupe, a simpleton

pink of perfection: the most perfect

pitched upon: selected

pleace: dialect for 'place'

pledge: drink a toast

postchaise: closed travelling-carriage conveying passengers from one stage (post) to another

post-coach: coach driven by horses hired from posting establishments

pound: enclosure for stray animals

presently: immediately

Prince Eugene: Prince of Savoy and famous Austrian general (1663–1736) who fought with Marlborough against the French in the War of the Spanish Succession

privy council: body of advisers to the monarch

puppy: impudent young fellow

quack: fake, charlatan

quarrelling for places: a passing reference to the political squabbles of the time; 'place' also meant a government appointment

quickset: hawthorn

Quis ... Quaes ... Quods: (Lat.) relative pronouns meaning 'who' and 'which'

quotha!: said he! (contemptuous)

rabbit me: confound me

'Rake's Progress': a series of prints by the artist William Hogarth (1697–1764), depicting the gradual ruin of a young man in pursuit of pleasure

rally: jest, tease

Ranelagh: fashionable area of London, though Ranelagh Gardens had a dubious reputation

rattle: prattle

receipt: remedy

reckoning: bill, account

regular: genuine, authentic

relics: the relics of saints and martyrs are, in many churches, holy objects of veneration and are rarely revealed

rose and table-cut: jewellery cut into sharp or smooth face

rule of thumb: rough and ready methods (i.e. here, by force)

rumpled: romped with

St James's: St James's Park; hence, highly fashionable

samplers: practice pieces of needlework

sartain: dialect for 'certain'

Scandalous Magazine: The Town and Country Magazine, which published gossip, rumour and scandal

scurvy: contemptible

sensible: sensitive, refined

sentiments: moral aphorisms

setting off: praising

shakebag: large fighting cock

shaking pudding: blancmange or jelly

side-box: in a theatre, a box close to the stage and so used by spectators who wanted to be conspicuous

slaves: i.e. the French, often so called before the French Revolution of 1789

smoked: galloped at speed

snub: to reprimand, to thwart

solus: (Lat.) alone

soused: pickled

spadille: card-game

spark: lover

speaking trumpet: precursor of the megaphone

spins the pewter platter: i.e. sings while keeping a plate spinning on its edge

spunk: spirit

staring: glaringly conspicuous

Stingo: a strong drink; hence, applied as a nickname to a landlord

tablets: notebook

taffety cream: smooth, thickened cream

take: understand

tête: elaborate headdress

tête-à-tête: (Fr.) a confidential conversation between two people. Also, in a magazine, an engraved portrait of a famous man's head with his mistress carrying a scandalous caption

'Tis not alone ... I've that within: reference to *Hamlet* (I, ii, 77 and 85)

Tower Wharf: district populated by thieves and vagabonds

town: London

track of the wheel: deep ruts left by carriage wheels in the hardened mud of rural lanes were dangerous for horses

trapesing, trolloping: ungainly, flaunting manner

trumpery: worthless trifles

varmint: vermin (i.e. his mother and cousin)

ventre d'or: (Fr.) gold-fronted

want: the word still retained its older sense of 'lack'

'Water Parted': song from the opera *Artaxerxes* by Thomas Arne (1710–78)

wauns: dialect for 'God's wounds', an oath

We wanted no ghost: i.e. 'that is obvious'; reference to *Hamlet* (I, v, 131)

Westminster Hall: then the site of the law courts in London

whimsical: odd, peculiar

whining end of a modern novel: i.e. implausibly coincidental, like the happy ending of a sentimental novel

Whistlejacket: famous racehorse

white and gold: i.e. white and gold coat and waistcoat

winding the straight horn: blowing a hunting horn

with a witness: with a vengeance

work: i.e. embroidery

'Would it were bed-time ...': a reference to Shakespeare's *1 Henry IV* (V, i, 125) where Falstaff is about to go unwillingly into battle

woundily: extremely

years of discretion: the age of twenty-one and over

zounds: a corruption of the oath 'by God's wounds'

Examination Questions

1. Read the following passage, and answer **all** the questions printed beneath it:

MARLOW. I'm so distracted with a variety of passions, that I don't know what I do. Forgive me, madam. George, forgive me. You know my hasty temper, and should not exasperate it.

HASTINGS. The torture of my situation is my only excuse.

MISS NEVILLE. Well, my dear Hastings, if you have that esteem for me 5
that I think, that I am sure you have, your constancy for three years will but increase the happiness of our future connection. If –

(*He embraces her.*)

MRS HARD. (*Within.*) Miss Neville. Constance, why, Constance, I say.

MISS NEVILLE. I'm coming. (*Releasing herself from Hastings' arms.*) Well, 10
constancy. (*Almost breaking down.*) Remember, constancy is the word.

(*She goes out, R., taking her cloak, etc., from the table.*)

HASTINGS. (*Distracted.*) My heart! How can I support this? To be so near happiness, and such happiness!

MARLOW. (*To Tony*) You see now, young gentleman, the effects of your 15
folly. What might be amusement to you, is here disappointment, and even distress.

TONY. (*Starting from his reverie.*) Ecod, I have hit it. It's here. Your hands. Yours and yours (*to Hastings*), my poor Sulky. (*Going to right, and calling.*) My boots there, ho! (*Turning to Hastings.*) Meet me two 20
hours hence at the bottom of the garden; and if you don't find Tony Lumpkin a more good natur'd fellow than you thought for, I'll give you leave to take my best horse, and Bet Bouncer into the bargain! Come along. (*Calling loudly.*) My boots, ho!   [*Exeunt.*

(i) What caused Marlow to be *so distracted with a variety of passions* (line 1) at this time? [4]

(ii) Explain how Hastings was *so near happiness* (lines 13–14), and how his plans were ruined. [6]

(iii) What have you learnt about *Bet Bouncer* (line 23)? How would she be affected by the success of Tony's plan (line 18)? [4]

(iv) Contrast the way Marlow, Hastings, and Constance speak with the way Tony speaks in this passage. [6]

2. In the play Marlow and Kate have four meetings. Without attempting to give a full and detailed account of each conversation, show how these move the plot forward to its happy conclusion.

(*Oxford Local Examinations*, 1980)

3. Read the following passage, and answer all the questions printed beneath it:

HARD. Pray, sir, as you take the house, what think you of taking the rest of the furniture? There's a pair of silver candlesticks and there's a firescreen and here's a pair of brazen-nosed bellows, perhaps you may take a fancy to them?

MARLOW. (*Rising.*) Bring me your bill, sir, bring me your bill, and let's make no more words about it. 5

HARD. There are a set of prints, too. What think you of 'The Rake's Progress' for your own apartment?

MARLOW. (*Angrily.*) Bring me your bill, I say; and I'll leave you and your infernal house directly. 10

HARD. Then there's a mahogany table, that you may see your own face in.

MARLOW. (*Furious.*) My bill, I say.

HARD. I had forgot the great chair, for your own particular slumbers, after a hearty meal. 15

MARLOW. (*Thundering at him.*) Zounds! bring me my bill, I say, and let's hear no more on't.

HARD. (*Coming forward.*) Young man, young man, from your father's letter to me, I was taught to expect a well-bred modest man, as a visitor here, but now I find him no better than a coxcomb and a bully; but he 20 will be down here presently, and shall hear more of it.

[*Exit abruptly.*

MARLOW. How's this. Sure, I have not mistaken the house? Everything looks like an inn. The servants cry 'coming'. The attendance is awkward; the barmaid, too, to attend us. 25

(*Enter Miss Hardcastle.*)
　　But she's here, and will further inform me.

　　(i) What was the immediate cause of Hardcastle's indignation
here?   [4]
　　(ii) Show, with some detail, how Hardcastle expresses this indignation.   [4]
　　(iii) What reasons, additional to those in lines 23–5, had Marlow for thinking
the house to be *an inn* (line 24)?   [4]
　　(iv) What did Marlow now learn from Kate to confirm his blunders? Explain
the confusion in Marlow's feelings towards Kate which he expresses in the
conversation which follows this extract.   [8]

　　4. **Either,** (*a*) Give an account of the part played by Kate Hardcastle in *She
Stoops to Conquer* and say what you learn about her character.

[20]

　　Or, (*b*) Discuss the relationship between Tony and Constance and show
how Tony contrives to thwart his mother's plans.   [20]
(*Oxford Local Examinations*, 1980)

　　5. Read the following passage, and answer **all** the questions printed beneath
it:

(*Enter Hastings and Miss Neville.*)
HASTINGS. My dear Constance, why will you deliberate thus? If we delay
　　a moment, all is lost for ever. Pluck up a little resolution, and we shall
　　soon be out of the reach of her malignity.
MISS NEVILLE. (*Miserably.*) I find it impossible. My spirits are so sunk
　　with the agitations I have suffered, that I am unable to face any new   5
　　danger. Two or three years' patience will at last crown us with happiness.
HASTINGS. Such a tedious delay is worse than inconstancy. Let us fly,
　　my charmer. Let us date our happiness from this very moment. Perish
　　fortune. Love and content will increase what we possess beyond a
　　monarch's revenue. Let me prevail.   10
MISS NEVILLE. No, Mr Hastings, no. Prudence once more comes to my
　　relief, and I will obey its dictates. In the moment of passion, fortune
　　may be despised, but it ever produces a lasting repentance. I'm resolved
　　to apply for Mr Hardcastle's compassion and justice for redress.
HASTINGS. But though he had the will, he has not the power to relieve   15
　　you.

MISS NEVILLE. But he has influence, and upon that I am resolved to
   rely.
HASTINGS. I have no hopes. But since you persist, I must reluctantly
   obey you.   [*Exeunt.*   20

   (i) To what does the phrase *her malignity* (line 3) refer? What had aroused
this malignity?   [5]
   (ii) Account for the difference between Hastings' state of mind and Constance's, at this time, by explaining what had been happening to each since
they last met.   [4]
   (iii) Show how this passage brings out the different natures of the two lovers.
                                                                   [4]
   (iv) Show that at the end of the play Mr Hardcastle had both *the will* and
the power to relieve Hastings and Miss Neville (lines 15–16).   [6]

   6. **Either,** (*a*) Write an account of the scene in the 'Three Pigeons' (Act 1,
Sc. 2) and show how it helps to advance the plot.   [20]
   Or, (*b*) Write an assessment of Marlow's character and say, with reasons,
whether you think he was the right husband for Kate or not.   [20]
                              (*Oxford Local Examinations*, 1981)

   7. Read the following passage, and answer **all** the questions printed beneath
it:

MARLOW. There again, may I be hanged, my dear, but I mistook you for
   the barmaid!
MISS HARD. (*With affected dignity.*) Dear me! dear me! I'm sure there's
   nothing in my *behaviour* to put me upon a level with one of that stamp.
MARLOW. Nothing, my dear, nothing. But I was in for a list of blunders,   5
   and could not help making you a subscriber. My stupidity saw everything the wrong way. I mistook your assiduity for assurance, and your
   simplicity for allurement. But it's over – this house I no more show *my*
   face in!
MISS HARD. I hope, sir, I have done nothing to disoblige you. I'm sure   10
   I should be sorry to affront any gentleman who has been so polite, and
   said so many civil things to me. I'm sure I should be sorry (*pretending
   to cry*) if he left the family upon my account. I'm sure I should be sorry
   people said anything amiss, since I have no fortune but my character.

MARLOW. (*Aside.*) By heaven, she weeps. This is the first mark of 15
tenderness I ever had from a modest woman, and it touches me. (*To her.*) Excuse me, my lovely girl, you are the only part of the family I leave with reluctance. But to be plain with you, the difference of our birth, fortune and education, make an honourable marriage impossible.

MISS HARD. But I'm sure my family is as good as Miss Hardcastle's, and 20
though I'm poor, that's no great misfortune to a contented mind, and, until this moment, I never thought that it was bad to want fortune.

MARLOW. And why now, my pretty simplicity?

MISS HARD. Because it puts me at a distance from one, that if I had a thousand pound I would give it all to. 25

MARLOW. (*Aside.*) This simplicity bewitches me, so that if I stay I'm undone. I must make one bold effort and leave her. (*To her.*) Your partiality in my favour, my dear, touches me most sensibly, and were I to live for myself alone, I could easily fix my choice. But I owe too much to the opinion of the world, too much to the authority of a father, 30
so that – I can scarcely speak it – it affects me! Farewell! (*Exit*)

(i) What happened on the occasion when Marlow *mistook* Kate for a *barmaid*? How did her *behaviour* (lines 1–2) on that occasion lead him to make his mistake? [6]

(ii) What is Kate pretending to be now? Show, by referring to her language and actions, that she is acting a part throughout this extract. [5]

(iii) What aspects of Marlow's character are revealed in this extract? Support your statements with evidence from the extract. [6]

(iv) Explain briefly how Marlow comes to propose to Kate. [3]

8. Tony tells Hastings and Marlow that finally they will find him 'a more good-natured fellow than they thought for'. Write an account of Tony's behaviour in the play bringing out his faults and his virtues.

(*Oxford Local Examinations*, 1981)